W. W Rawson

Success in market-gardening

a new vegetable growers' manual. Seventh Edition

W. W Rawson

Success in market-gardening
a new vegetable growers' manual. Seventh Edition

ISBN/EAN: 9783337374525

Printed in Europe, USA, Canada, Australia, Japan

Cover: Foto ©Lupo / pixelio.de

More available books at **www.hansebooks.com**

SUCCESS IN MARKET GARDENING

A NEW

VEGETABLE GROWERS' MANUAL

BY

W. W. RAWSON

OF ARLINGTON, MASS.

Seventh Edition

*REVISED AND ENLARGED, WITH NEW MATTER
AND ILLUSTRATIONS*

BOSTON, MASS.:
PUBLISHED BY THE AUTHOR
1892

COPYRIGHT, 1892,
BY W. W. RAWSON.

Electrotyped and Printed By
CASHMAN, KEATING & CO., BOSTON.

PREFACE.

IN view of the rapid changes and improvements in varieties and modes of culture which continually appear, it must be evident that the practical rules of Market Gardening need to be frequently revised and brought down to date; and any Manual on this subject, to be of practical value to the reader, must include many important directions not hitherto found in works of this class. Except the earlier editions of the present work, no treatise within my knowledge has appeared for a very considerable time that has aimed at covering the field with any approach to completeness; and, moreover, so far as I am aware, no other work has ever yet been written that is fully adapted to the latitude of New England. Five years have gone by since its first publication, within which time the products and modes of culture have been varied and developed to such an extent as to call for corresponding revisions and extensions of its contents.

I have been brought up in the business of Market Gardening. My father followed it before me, and, being led to it both by circumstances and inclination, I naturally took it up. I must have had a strong predilection for the work or I should not have followed it, as I have, continuously until now. I can now point back to a successful business experience of twenty-five years and more, on a continually increasing scale; and believe no Market Gardener in Massachusetts or New England has at any time employed a larger capital, or marketed a larger annual product, than I now do.

The extent of my establishment and operations at Arlington has attracted general public notice. Men who have already embarked in the business, and have themselves been more or less successful in it, will find in this book the means of comparing their own methods with mine. Young men who are about to choose their avocation, and who have heard of the increasing extent and importance of this business of Vegetable Growing, will find here facts collected from a long experience, which can hardly fail to be valuable to an attentive reader.

A reasonable man will estimate the worth of this book by what it contains — not criticising it for the absence of matters which lie beyond its scope and purpose. In the introductory remarks with which it opens, I have endeavored to explain my object with sufficient precision, and throughout the preparation of the work I have aimed to outdo, rather than come short of, the promise held forth in the opening chapter.

The revisions and enlargements which may be found in the present edition illustrate the most recent changes and improvements in the art of Market Gardening.

W. W R.

ARLINGTON, MASS., *January*, *1892*.

CONTENTS.

PART I.— *On the Growing of Crops in General.*

CHAPTER I.

INTRODUCTORY REMARKS.— Scope of the Work 9–10
LOCATION AND SOIL.— Choice of a Location.— Convenience of Slopes.
— Character of Soil 11–14
LAND DRAINAGE.— Construction of Drains.— Provision for Outlet.—
Depths and Intervals.— Benefits 15–20
IRRIGATION. — Necessity for Watering. — Sub-irrigation. — Surface
Waterings. — Sources of Supply. — Storage. — Amount and Frequency.— Distributing by Hose.— Service of the Pump.— Outfit and
Operation.— Estimates of Cost.— Instances of Success.— Further
Instructions 21–32

CHAPTER II.

PREPARATION OF THE SOIL.— First Stages.— How to Plow.— A
Thorough Tillage 33–37
LAYING OUT CROPS AND ROTATION.— Systematic Work.— Objects
of a Rotation 38–41
MANURES AND FERTILIZERS.— Amounts and Methods.— Sources of
the Supply.— Overhauling and Distributing on Land.— Processes
of Fermentation.— Commercial Fertilizers.— Night Soil.— Wood
Ashes.— Manuring in the Hill.— Composts.— Liquid Manures.—
Comparative Values.— Chemical Constituents.— Works of Reference 42–53
APPLICATION OF MANURES.— Rapid-Growing Crops.— Fertilizing
Land under Crop.— Different Methods 54–56

CHAPTER III.

SELECTION OF SEEDS.— Growing or Purchasing.— Best is Cheapest.—
When to Purchase.— Testing for Quality 57–58
VITALITY OF SEEDS.— How Impaired.— How Preserved.— Continuance of Vitality.— Growth from Fresh or Older Seeds . . . 59–60
SEED-GROWING.— By Vegetable-Growers.— By Seedsmen.— Improving
the Strain.— Differences in Maturing.— Arlington Seed-Growing.—
Best is Cheapest.— Gathering and Curing 61–62
SOWING THE SEED — In Newly Worked Soil.— Depth and Other Conditions 63–6
CULTIVATION OF CROPS.— During Growth.— Other Rules and Suggestions 65–66
CONSTRUCTION AND OPERATION OF HOT-BEDS — Furnishing and Regulating the Heat.— Continuous Care Essential.— Temperature and
Other Conditions of Success.— Four Crops in a Season . . . 67–70

v

CONTENTS.

	PAGE
GARDENING IN HOT-Houses.— Growth of the Practice.— Advantages Resulting.— Requirements for Heating	71-72
GATHERING THE CROPS.— When to Gather.— Handling and Packing	73-74
CAPITAL AND LABOR.— Amounts Required.— Practices and Opinions. — Rules and Data.— Cost of Sundry Items	75-76

PART II. — Special Crops, Tools, and Various Requisites.

CHAPTER IV.

VEGETABLES RAISED FOR MARKET.— Characteristics of, and Cultural Directions for, the following kinds : — Artichoke— Jerusalem Artichoke — Asparagus — Dwarf or Bush Beans — Pole Beans — Scarlet Runners — Lima Beans — Beets — Borecole, or Kale — Broccoli — Brussels Sprouts — Cabbage — Carrots — Cauliflower — Celeriac — Celery — Chicory — Chives 79-123

CHAPTER V.

VEGETABLES RAISED FOR MARKET.— Characteristics, etc., *Continued.* Field Corn — Sweet Corn — Corn Salad — Cress — Upland Cress — Cucumbers — Dandelion — Egg Plant — Endive — Herbs — Horse Radish — Kohl Rabi — Leek — Lettuce — Martynia — Mushrooms — Muskmelons and Cantaloupes — Mustard — Nasturtium — Okra 124-160

CHAPTER VI.

VEGETABLES RAISED FOR MARKET.— Characteristics, etc., *Continued.* Onions — Parsley — Parsnips — Peas — Peppers — Potatoes — Radishes — Rhubarb — Salsify — Spinach — Squash — Tomatoes — Turnips — Watermelons — Chinese Yam 161-202

CHAPTER VII.

IMPLEMENTS, ORDINARY AND SPECIAL.— Kemp's Manure Spreader — Plows — Useful Styles — Harrows — Rollers — Cultivators — Small Tools — Wheel Hoes — Seed-Drills — Combination Wheel Tools — Tools for Special Uses 203-218
GREENHOUSES, ETC. — Modes of Heating — Use of Electric Light — Permanent Outside Beds — Low Cost Forcing House . . 219-222
PUMPING OUTFITS.— Different Styles— Various Kinds of Power . 223-226
INSECT PESTS.— Preventives— Process of Fumigation . . . 227-233
FUNGI AND PLANT DISEASES.— Nature and Growth of Fungi— Preventives — Process of Spraying 233-237
IN CONCLUSION.— Practice vs. Theory— Experiments and Results — Forcing-House Products — Closing Suggestions . . . 238-240

SUCCESS IN MARKET GARDENING.

Part I.

ON THE GROWING OF CROPS IN GENERAL.

SUCCESS IN MARKET GARDENING.

CHAPTER I.

INTRODUCTORY REMARKS — LOCATION AND SOILS — LAND DRAINAGE — IRRIGATION OF CROPS — ESTIMATES OF COST — INSTRUCTIONS.

MARKET GARDENING as a business has some peculiar features in which it differs from other branches of agriculture. Many people have an impression that the growing of vegetables for market is like any ordinary farming, and are disposed to believe that any person who can plough, hoe, and dig can grow one crop as well as another. Such people would find themselves sadly mistaken if they should undertake the business themselves and actually attempt to carry it on equipped with only a general knowledge of ordinary farm work.

Market gardening is made up of details; and, while each separate step may be easy of mastery by those who have a natural taste for the business, the whole art and a full comprehension of it can be acquired only by actual experience in the work and thorough practical acquaintance with all the minor points.

Therefore we desire every one to understand at the outset that a book on the subject, no matter how complete, can be only a helper, and a partial guide towards the desired knowledge. In other words, the rules that can be laid down on paper, however explicit they may be made, will never educate a man to be a successful gardener, unless he is himself naturally adapted to the business, and is willing to do his part by personally devoting himself to the work, in all its details, as it goes along.

And so in writing the cultural directions for the different crops, I do not expect to be explicit enough to enable a mere novice, with no knowledge whatever of the subject, to achieve a success in gardening the first year. This would be impossible for me to do, were I to attempt it — which I do not. Even should I set down the most minute particulars and details, there would be very few cases where one could carry them out to the letter, as culture and treatment must necessarily vary according to soil and locality.

But my aim is simply this : by writing out practical directions and descriptions, gathered from my own experience, to enable any one, already in some degree familiar with the work, to cultivate successfully the various crops enumerated; provided his land and location are adapted to them. I propose to give my readers, as far as possible, the benefit of my own practical experience, and the methods of a success in business which has been gained only by years of close application and hard work.

In the following pages, I shall discuss at more or less length all the different products of the market garden; and some of the coarser crops, belonging rather to the "farm garden," or even to the farm, will be incidentally treated of. In so doing, I shall go through the whole series in alphabetical order, in order that the reader may the more readily turn to the information he is seeking. I propose to devote space most liberally to the most important crops. A chapter on Farm Implements and other supplementary matter will conclude the work.

But there are certain conditions essential to all crops. Some of the most essential requirements of high cultivation, and even of the most ordinary soil-culture, are often misconceived or overlooked, to a serious extent. For which reason it seems best, before proceeding to particular directions for particular crops, to treat, as fully as space will permit, of these general and very essential matters.

LOCATION AND SOILS.

In seeking a good location for a market garden, of course the first point to be taken into consideration is the necessity of being near some good market.

And, right here, we would say that the largest cities do not always offer the greatest inducements to beginners. There are hundreds of wide-awake towns all over the country which will furnish a good, though limited, market for men who are able to work up a trade.

In these smaller towns, producers will often be enabled to realize better prices than in metropolitan markets, both from the fact that there is less competition to meet, and also because the purchasers there found will be likely to look more to the quality, and less to the cheapness, of the article offered, than those resorting to the city markets.

As we have mentioned, nearness to market is an important point, but the character of the soil and the lay of the land are of importance almost as vital as location. Of course, for a variety of crops, the land should be varied in character. But such variety cannot always be obtained, so that many are confined to one or two distinct kinds of soil, and in such cases find themselves limited to such few crops as are particularly adapted to their land and location.

Rocky ground is of course and by all means to be avoided for garden crops, in view of the deep and uniform cultivation they need to receive. And low lands which require under-draining are adapted only to certain special crops, and involve heavy outlays to make them capable of profitable culture. Preferably to either, a sandy loam with a sandy or gravelly subsoil should be selected. Such land is far better than soils resting on clay, not only because its nature is warmer, but because it is naturally well drained. A clay subsoil, at least until deep drains have been sunk and operated a considerable time, will render any land cold, as it retains the moisture.

If one can have his choice as regards the lay of his land, gently rolling or undulating slopes with a general eastern or southern exposure should by all means be selected. This will make more difference than some might imagine; as a northern or western slope is not nearly so soon affected by the genial spring influences as a more sunny location.

The difference between a northern and a southern slope often amounts to one crop a year; for on the sunny side of a rise of land the soil can be worked in the spring so much earlier that, by right calculation, two crops a year can be grown, the first of which can be planted earlier—and the second can actually be harvested sooner—than the one crop raised on a northern slope.

Sloping land has still another advantage, almost equally desirable with that derived from having the right exposure, consisting in the facility it affords for irrigation. If a water supply can be brought to and stored in a tank, constructed on a natural elevation within the area to be irrigated, the slopes of course furnish the most convenient means possible for its distribution to the crops. And if the location is fortunately near a large pond, or unfailing brook, the privilege of access to such a water supply would very greatly increase the real value of the land for every sort of cultivation.

It should be noticed that some ground which in its native condition is quite incapable of bearing good crops has yet a superior *natural capacity*, that may be developed by skilful handling and liberal expenditure. This is especially true of lands lying on a retentive subsoil, and such lands, after some years of thorough draining and deep tilth, will show admirable results. In treating of drainage, we shall endeavor to make it clear how such a course of culture operates to mellow and warm the cold, barren soils, and bring them into high condition. In fact—having a good exposure to begin with — by drainage, deep tilth, generous and judicious manuring, and irrigation as required, the most barren spot on earth can be made as highly productive as any other soil, even the richest. It is only a question of time and expense. Accordingly it has been said, not without some truth, that after all the chief matter in choosing a location is its convenience to markets of sale and supply; because if the soil be never so unfavorable the owner can make it over to suit himself, while if he is remote from market he can do nothing to help himself as regards that difficulty. All these considerations have weight, and must be duly allowed for; but the point I desire most to insist upon is the advantages possessed by the loams lying on sandy or gravelly subsoils, in their excellent natural drainage, and in being easy of cultivation.

LAND DRAINAGE.

Land, Soil, or Agricultural Drainage is a topic already touched upon, because inevitably presenting itself in connection with the choice of a proper location; but it is quite too large a subject to be dismissed with a brief and merely casual mention.

In selecting a location for either market gardening or farming, it is preferable, as we have said, to secure land that is *naturally* well drained. By this description we designate a soil which, owing to inclination of surface, or from having a porous subsoil, lets the water pass off quickly after a heavy rainfall, and which therefore stands in no need of artificial drainage. But it is not always possible to secure such a location, and in many cases artificial drainage is the only means by which the best of farming land can be brought under cultivation.

It would be impossible in a volume of this size, even if wholly devoted to the topic, to give a complete description, with all details of methods and materials employed, for constructing the tile drains now in general use. We can only hope to give a few detached suggestions on the subject, such as may be of benefit to our readers in improving waste land, and in rendering heavy, soggy fields more tillable, and turning to account their natural fertility.

Amongst all the various ways of constructing permanent drains — with stone, brush, square and sole tile, etc.— it has become the well established general opinion that well-burned round tiles, with collars, if well laid, form the best. And in the long run they also prove the cheapest; although at first more expensive than some other devices.

Cobble-stone drains, such as in some localities are largely used in place of tile, are, when properly laid, actually more costly. And still more objectionable is the fact that, although in some instances they may last a long time and prove quite serviceable, they are always liable to be reached by surface water, which, by carrying silt into them, stops them up, and of course renders them useless.

The general principles to be observed in laying a stone drain are quite well understood. But a mistake is often made by lack of diligence in securing proper covering, and especially by resorting to the use of turf, which is often dumped in upon the stones, and which, when decayed, forms the most effective possible material for obstructing the drain.

There are many ways of constructing cheap drains of brush, slabs, poles, etc., but they are sure to clog up and create trouble sooner or later; and, as we have said before, the round tile when well laid, generally speaking, forms the cheapest and most satisfactory means of draining.

In planning for the draining of a field, the chiefly important item is to take notice of the lowest point; at which the outlet must be formed. If a natural watercourse can be found near by, as much as four or five feet lower than the lowest surface of the field, it will be a great saving, both as regards expense and trouble. The ditch by which the water is carried from the outlet must be of sufficient capacity to serve its purpose at all times and seasons in a thoroughly adequate manner.

The laying out of mains, sub-mains, and laterals must depend wholly upon the character and condition of the land. More skill is required to lay out properly a complicated system of drains than to conduct any other branch of the gardener's work; and the designing of it is a more puzzling matter than people generally realize, until they have had some experience in it.

In the brief space which we can give to the subject it is impossible to describe minutely the methods of mapping out such a system; and we cannot do better, therefore, than to refer our readers to George E. Waring, Jr.'s able work on "Draining for Profit and Draining for Health," which is the most complete work on this subject with which we are acquainted. Any one who has even a moderate amount of this class of improvements in contemplation ought by all means to possess a copy of the above named book, and make himself master of its contents by careful and diligent study.

The author recommends a general depth of four feet for drains; never admitting a less depth unless where an outlet at that depth cannot be obtained, or where ground is underlaid by rock. There is a general concurrence of opinion amongst those who have most carefully examined the subject, favoring this rule for the least depth. At intermediate points occurring between such (minimum) depths, the depth must be often greater, because the drain must slope uniformly from point to point, while the land does not.

As regards the distance between the drains, there is a difference of opinion, in fact this is a question which does not admit of any exact or definite solution, as it obviously depends in a great degree upon the peculiar constitution of the soil, which is variable; and, moreover, no amount of practical experience even will afford data for reducing practice to any well-grounded theoretical rule. It is not feasible to state, in exact terms, precisely what is the operation of these subterranean drains upon the moisture of the soil; but an idea sufficiently definite for all practical purposes may be gathered from experience.

In tolerably porous soils, forty or even fifty feet apart is generally conceded to be sufficiently near for four-foot drains. But for the more retentive clays, all distances from eighteen feet to fifty have been recommended. The feeling grows more in favor of the greater width, from continued observation of the successful working of drains so placed. Still the author's opinion, formed from over twenty years of personal experience and observation of such works, and with due consideration of views published by others, is that we should hardly ever, where a soil needs draining at all, leave widths exceeding forty feet.

He further says that, in the lighter loams, there has been good success in following Prof. Mapes' rule: that "three-foot drains should be placed twenty feet apart, and for each additional foot in depth the distance may be doubled. For instance, four-foot drains may be forty feet apart, and five-foot drains eighty feet apart." But with reference to this greater distance,—eighty feet,—it is not to be recommended in stiff clays for any depth of drain. When it is necessary, on account of underlying rock or by reason of insufficient fall, to go only three feet deep, the drains should be as near together as twenty feet

No great exactness can be had in such a matter as this. In consideration of the variety of soils, and our inability to measure the exact amount of water to be drawn off (which is never a constant quantity), or even the rate at which it may reach the drains by percolation through any given soil, uniform depths and distances cannot of course be prescribed with any pretence to theoretical precision. A general judgment made up from experience and observation is all that can be offered.

GOOD RESULTS OF DRAINING.

For explanation of the beneficial influences of draining, we must endeavor to realize some of the conditions of plant life. One of these is moisture at the roots. If drainage were attended by a complete withdrawal of all the permanent moisture of the soil, no one would be its advocate. Some imagine that wherever executed it is to the detriment of the land's *capacity for production*, though increasing its capacity for *being cultivated*. They say "more tillable is not more fertile. Tile draining is a craze. Wholesale rules without discrimination are a curse. Drained lands are not invariably better than the same lands undrained," etc.

But we maintain that in all soils not naturally well-drained (and so not requiring it) draining does as much good by promoting moisture during periods of drought, as by removal of the surplus water, which would otherwise destroy the productive capacity of the land. This is due to the fact that the deeper tilth and pulverization of the drained lands enable them to hold in saturation, as water is held in a sponge, valuable stores of water to be given off a little at a time, as needed, and also to draw up from below, by capillary attraction, similar timely supplies — while all excess and surplus is promptly gotten rid of.

A recently published work by A. N. Cole contains suggestions of interest in this connection. We have suggested that the most perfect drainage does not aim at a complete withdrawal of all the moisture; water is essential to plant life, but the land must not be *drowned* with water. Air and water both must be presented to the feeding roots. He says, "tilled land being porous, the air forces its way into the crevices, and the water (of rains) passes through it from above. We will suppose that the water comes to a stratum that is impervious to its onward course. What happens? Simply this: it dams up slowly, inch by inch, forcing out the air as it rises. All motion and circulation is stopped. Fermentation and decomposition soon begin. The earth is drowned out — suffocated — dead for want of air. Water is good for the ground? Yes; but not in this way. The water must be moving constantly. There must be a current of air and water, and not too much or too little of the latter."

The processes of pulverization, which will be described under the title "Preparation of Soil," are such as to provide for the admission of the air. We shall now consider, in the remainder of the present chapter, by what means we may supply the needful amount of the other indispensable element, water. By drainage we provide for the removal of a surplus, whether from rains or springs; our next care must be for supply and distribution of a quantity adequate, in the longest and severest droughts, to the exacting needs of the growing crops. This supply and distribution constitute what is intended by the term "Irrigation."

IRRIGATION OF CROPS.

Artificial watering, especially as now conducted, forms perhaps one of the most important subjects that we could write upon. All vegetables are composed largely of water, some containing more than 75 per cent. A single hill of cucumbers, as has been said, will drink half a barrelful of water in three days' time, and, having done so, will begin languishing for lack of moisture, and die in a week. According to Dr. J. H. Gilbert, for every ton of dry substance grown, in an average crop, an amount of water equivalent to three inches of rain is exhaled in the process; which amounts to about two hundred times the weight of the vegetable product. And Sir J. B. Lawes arrived at substantially the same result by his own researches, separately prosecuted. Hence it will be readily seen that, unless there is moisture enough when the crop requires it, there will be a shortage in the harvest.

What is commonly called an "impoverished soil," or one considered naturally unfertile, may be in fact good enough in itself, its only deficiency being in the matter of moisture. We often see a poor piece of land yielding a good crop in a wet season; and artificial watering on the grand scale has, in many well known instances in Colorado, California, and elsewhere, both at home and abroad, converted absolute deserts into productive grain farms and fruit and cattle ranches.

Although the rainfall during each year averages about the same now as in former periods, the seasons are changing in this respect: that the rainfall is not so evenly divided, and we get longer and more protracted droughts; not relieved by the fact that the rainfalls, when they do come, are heavier. For this reason the subject of irrigation is constantly gaining in importance. It involves questions, both in regard to the supply of water and the manner of applying it. Of course there are many cases where land is not located so as to be easily irrigated. Whatever the location is, no matter if quite favorable, it will require careful management in laying out the rows and planting the crops, to secure a plan which will allow of irrigating to the best advantage. The rows should always run up and down the slope of ground, and more or less obliquely if the ground is at all steep (instead of crossway), so as to allow of watering in the furrow, which is the proper way, as the moisture is required to be applied to the roots and not the foliage.

One excellent method of applying moisture to the soil consists in sending water through lines of tiles properly laid in the ground, with joints slightly open between each tile and the next one — a method mostly practised on low lands. The distribution of the moisture is accomplished very successfully, by stopping the lowest end of each line of tiles and filling into it from the highest point. This method I would recommend for low and heavy lands; because if water were to be applied to the surface, the soil would harden and an injury to the growing crop would result. On sandy lands the largest benefit will be derived by running it over the surface about once a week; applying about one inch at a time, which is above the average quantity resulting from a good rainfall in our New England climate.

When the rainfalls are of average amount and come with uniformity, no addition by way of irrigation is required; but when, as is very often the case, no rain falls for two or three weeks or more, it may become necessary to make two or three applications. Irrigation by watering the foliage is not recommended, except under glass, where it is often necessary, and can be applied without injury to the growing crop.

It is better to water under glass on a pleasant day than on a stormy or cloudy one; but in the field a cloudy one would be preferred, if the water was to be applied so as to wet the foliage.

There are numerous Market Gardeners at the present time who have abundant facilities for supplying themselves with water for irrigation; though it has only been secured, ordinarily, by a liberal outlay.

Although many places are located near towns or cities which have a public water supply, they cannot be allowed to draw from the supply in such large quantities as are required for purposes of irrigation, as the need would come at a time when the water was the lowest in the reservoir, and was most in demand for other purposes. It is, therefore, necessary that the land to be irrigated should be located near a pond, lake, or stream, or resort must be had to under currents of water that may be reached by a driven well.

I much prefer to pump from wells in all cases, because in the summer the water from ponds or rivers is quite warm, while that from wells is cool, and this coolness will be an advantage to the crop, especially if the ground is very dry and hot, as is often the case; and again in winter, if taken from ponds or rivers, is very cold, and could not be put upon the plants until it had been warmed, while that taken from wells would be at a proper temperature to be applied immediately.

For these reasons I have always preferred the wells; and have always used them.

Appliances for pumping sometimes comprise windmills, and sometimes steam power is used; but for those who can afford the outlay, it is much the best to have both. The cheapest pumping is done by the windmill; but when it does not pump a sufficient quantity, then the steam-pump can be used. In many places there are elevated ponds or rivers that can be caused to flow by gravity to the point desired, either through closed conduits or pipes, or in open canals; when such is the case, no pumping is necessary.

After a sufficient supply of water is found, and a method of raising it to a proper height for distribution, — by the use either of steam-pumps or windmills, or both — a tank or reservoir of the largest attainable capacity must next be provided for the purpose of storing the water so raised until it can be properly distributed to the crops. Where windmills are used, for obvious reasons, the storage capacity must be greater than where steam-pumps are employed. This may amount to a considerable addition to the first cost; but, on the other hand, the cost of steam-pump and boiler is somewhat greater, and the running expenses considerably so. There are incidental advantages attending the use of steam which may be of great importance. The preference must depend upon one's situation; as above said, it will pay to have both.

The expense of fitting up such an arrangement for irrigating a market garden is not so large that gardeners should say they cannot afford it. At present prices and in the light of our present experience, we can reckon the cost at figures much lower than five years ago. If one has not the means to pay for these facilities, and does not feel warranted in going into debt for what he wants, of course he must do without them, and depend on transient watering from summer showers. But it becomes more and more evident every year that such a course will ruin the man who follows it. The ill effects of the increasing irregularity of the rainfall are mitigated, it is true, by deeper ploughing and the construction of drainage works, but all crops (some more than others), in addition to every other aid that can be given them, will need besides, at certain times, abundant watering. Even in the most favorable seasons, resort must be had to artificial watering at intervals, to secure the growing and maturing of a crop such as to give satisfaction, and reward the gardener for his labor.

Unfortunately we do not know from one day to another what weather to expect, whether a deluge or a drought. We are in constant fear lest the shower that comes to-day may be the last for a month; yet we have to put the water on lightly for fear there may be a deluge the next day. One inch of water at any one time is all that it is safe to apply. If there is no rain for a week, then another inch; and so on through the season, as the necessity appears. I think that one inch of water over the surface once a week will keep any crop growing in the driest weather.

A good steam-pump will supply that amount over one acre of land through a three-inch pipe in six hours.

For about nine months of the year a windmill would furnish all the water required by a market garden, but during the other three months a steam-pump would be required in addition in order to furnish a sufficient supply for all seasons.

On a later page we shall present a cut of a compact and serviceable steam apparatus designed for pumping, under Deane's patent. It combines all the essential features needed for drawing water from the source of supply (well, spring, stream, pond, or tank), and forcing the water any distance and height to a point suitable for distributing it, by gravity, over the land to be irrigated; or, as frequently practised, forcing it through pipes to hydrants, where hose can be used for further distribution. In some cases the hose may run directly from the pump. It is much more easily understood and managed than might be supposed, owing to the simplicity and compact style of its construction. It is claimed to be the simplest arrangement of the kind on the market, and such that any one of ordinary intelligence can learn to operate it in half a day.*

The easiest and often the best way of leading the water to various localities at will is by the use of rubber hose; this is cheaper than pipe, which is heavy, and very awkward to handle. It is often found practicable to obtain rejected steam fire-engine hose which, although not strong enough to stand the pressure of the steam fire-engines, is amply strong enough to use for irrigating. There is seldom more than thirty pounds' pressure, as the water is not forced, but is allowed to run through the open hose. The amount

* Consult Chapter VII.

of land that can be irrigated by the use of a steam-pump in a day of twelve hours is about three acres. By using a suitable pump we can throw one hundred gallons per minute, which, in a day of twelve hours, would be equivalent to covering three acres more than seven-eighths of an inch deep; equivalent in quantity to what we should call an abundant fall of rain; — indeed, it is rather more than an average of rainfalls, and certainly we cannot believe there is ever an acre of growing crop which, in a dry time, would not be benefited by such a watering to an amount much more than the cost; though many people shrink from the expense involved, and are skeptical about getting full return for the outlay.

But certainly where water can be had in ample quantity, and can be applied at such moderate cost as may be inferred from the foregoing statements, it must be plain to every one, and, practically, every one does now believe that it will and does pay, in frequent instances earning many times over the amount it costs. It has often times occurred that such a watering, once or oftener applied, has saved a crop that, without it, would have been a complete failure. For my part, I would as soon think of being without a steam-pump as the farmer who cuts hay would of being without a mowing-machine.

There is very seldom a season so wet that the steam-pump will not be required two or three weeks; and in most seasons it will be in use eight or ten weeks. When the weather is very dry, and all the crops need abundant watering, the pump should be kept running night and day, by employing two sets of men. It will be economy to do this, not only from the fact that a double supply is thus obtained, but because when the fire is allowed to go out at night it takes about an hour to get the pump to running again. By continuous running, time is saved at both ends of the day.

Be sure to provide a good pump, one that will pump at least seventy and better if one hundred gallons per minute. I do not recommend the smaller pump, for it will cost just as much to run one of the small size, except for a trifling difference in the quantity of coal required; and the price of a large pump is not much more than that of a small one, while it will do many times the work with the same labor.

It takes one man to run the pump and one to attend to the hose. Only a very little hose will be required, if the land is well piped in the manner following, viz.: I would advise beginning the piping with two and one-half inch cement-lined pipe placed under ground with hydrants set but a short distance apart. Run one such line from the tank-supply main fed by the mill or pump, as the case may be, to each of the buildings and hot-beds; and pipe for all the outside culture with three-inch pipe of the same class carried above ground, and furnished with faucets suitable for attaching hose at intervals, so arranged that the distance in any direction from each faucet to the next shall not exceed seventy-five or eighty feet. This surface-pipe must be taken up each year in the fall and replaced every spring.

Such arrangements may appear rather expensive,

but it will save much time in the busy season to have the water carried to all parts of the place. On a place of ten acres, the cost of putting in pump, boiler, pipes, and fittings need not be over $1,000. I had rather have a place of ten acres well fitted up for irrigation, than one of twenty without irrigation; and I venture the assertion that I could raise more vegetables, or receive more money for my crops, in a period of ten years, from the ten acres irrigated, than from the twenty acres not irrigated.

Any farm that has been well equipped for irrigation, whether it be one or five, ten or twenty acres, will bring enough more at any time, when offered for sale, to pay for the amount so expended. Therefore, the expense, beyond fuel, labor, and repairs, would be only the annual interest on the cost. We will allow $50.00 for interest, or $5.00 per acre on ten acres. The direct cost of running pump for twenty-four hours continuously, would consist of the following items: Coal, $3.00; skilled labor, including repairs, $7.00; additional help in moving hose, $2.00; making a total of $12.00, to which add, for wear and tear, $2.00; then we have $14.00 as the cost, exclusive of interest, for each watering of six acres; or $2.33 per acre.

But the total interest charge remaining unchanged, whatever the number of waterings made in a season, has to be borne in equal shares by all the waterings. The resulting cost for a single watering only might be as high as $7.33 per acre, if it were the only one made that season; but if two applications are made, the cost drops to $4.83 per acre. In the case of three, the resulting cost for each one will amount only to $4.00 per acre; and, where there are four, only $3.58.

In the foregoing calculation we have reckoned on the pump as discharging one hundred gallons a minute. The seventy-gallon pump would, substantially, do the watering of only four acres, instead of six, within the time computed for, with but an imperceptible amount of saving on the total cost of the day's operations.

The practice of irrigating by the aid of pipes and hydrants has only lately been introduced here, and owing to the great outlay involved, the method is used by comparatively few. But too much cannot be said in favor of irrigation; and the use of windmills and steam-pumps has become well-nigh universal.*

In one instance, which was reported to the Massachusetts Horticultural Society, in a severe drought, a steam-pump was rigged, and the water of Mystic River was poured for seven days and nights upon a parched field, averaging 75,000 gallons per day, or a quantity equal to three inches over the entire surface, at a cost, including all expenses, of perhaps ten cents per 1,000 gallons.

Somewhat later, in 1884, the present writer had six acres planted with cauliflowers. This is a crop which does not show the effect of dry weather until about to head; when, if there is danger of a check, the application of water will cause them to go right on. That year the need was urgent, and he devoted his steam-pump to the work of supply — running it continuously for four weeks, with two men by day and two to relieve them at night. From these six acres he sold $3,500

* Consult Chapter VII.

worth of cauliflowers. If he had not irrigated them he would not, probably, have realized over $1,000 for his crop. Very many similar instances might be given.

In applying the water to a field of cabbages or cauliflowers, the rows being about three and a half feet apart, a plough is run between the rows, so as to make a furrow for the water to run in. It is a very easy matter to water a field where the land is on a slope, but where it is nearly level it is much more work, as the hose has to be frequently transferred to different points in order to water evenly.

In watering a field of celery a furrow is ploughed *away* from the plants, on each side of the row, at a distance of about one foot. The furrow is then filled with water; and as soon as this has soaked away the furrow is turned back again. An application of this kind once a week will prove sufficient even in the driest time.

It will be manifest, upon reflection, that continuous light waterings are not what is desired. Water cannot, of course, be applied without reducing the temperature of the soil very materially, and thus occasioning, for the time, a condition unfavorable to the advance of the crop. This is a matter for serious consideration, in connection with many crops, especially in a climate like ours. In the case of light waterings, frequently repeated, a larger proportion disappears by immediate evaporation, thus wasting work, and, moreover, by this excessive evaporation, still further and needlessly reducing the temperature of the soil. Liberal supplies at proper intervals are rather to be given, transferring

the delivery from one section of the grounds
another, on successive days, and so continuing till
is time to resume the round. The proper interval
in a time of drought, may be taken to be about o1
week, on the average,—though this must vary wi'
the crop, the soil, the temperature, and the judgme
of the cultivator. The same variation may be e:
pected in estimating the amount of water necessa:
for one thorough irrigation. No general estimate c
these points can be given that will be at all satisfa
tory, except merely as a rough rule for planning tl
scale of the works. In establishing such a system, r
great nicety of calculation is likely to be of any valu
The data already given, and the practical exampl
which have been cited, will enable any one, making di
allowance for variations of circumstances, to arrive
a conclusion near enough for his purposes.

CHAPTER II.

PREPARATION OF THE SOIL—LAYING OUT OF LAND
FOR THE DIFFERENT CROPS—ROTATION OF CROPS
—MANURES—THEIR APPLICATION.

A PROPER PREPARATION of the soil, prior to sowing or planting, is one of the most important conditions involved in the process of getting a crop. We shall not aim to discuss at length the principles on which it depends, but confine ourselves in the main to simple and practical directions as to the work to be done.

Ploughing, subsoiling, harrowing, raking, and (at some stage of the process) manuring,—these constitute the main operations by which the land, after being stripped of a crop, is put into condition to be planted with another.

For all market-garden crops we recommend that the ground be ploughed once before an application of manure is made. In the case of all leaf crops, like celery, cabbage, etc., eight inches would be a sufficient depth for this first ploughing, before the manure is applied. For the second ploughing, which is to turn the manure under, a depth of six inches would be sufficient, and preferable : so as to leave the manure as near the surface as possible, and still have it covered.

Then, if the land is lumpy or hard, a wheel harrow or some implement for breaking up the lumps should be put to service. Lumpy, uneven ground, or coarse soil will never do to plant in: seeds will not catch uniformly or grow well in it; the plants will lack uniformity, and will not mature together. The importance of this matter is too generally underrated; very few people have anything like an adequate idea of it. If the ground is to be devoted to raising greens, or some sowed crop where a drill is to be employed, a Meeker harrow will smooth the surface nicely, so that the seed-sower will do its work to satisfaction. A full description of its operation may be found in the chapter treating of Farming Implements.

This harrow will prepare the surface sufficiently well for such crops as onions, cabbages, or beets, and for spinach and other sorts of greens; but for such small fine seeds as those of lettuce, or dandelion, the hand rake must be brought into service.

For root crops, at the first ploughing a depth of twelve inches would be none too much. In ploughing for deep-rooted crops, like parsnips, long carrots, or horseradish, the second ploughing should be of eight inches' depth; and this should be followed by a "subsoil," after which use the Meeker harrow or leveller, as already directed.

After ploughing and harrowing, it is often advisable to pass the roller over the land. The horse roller is a very useful article, and is used very extensively. When the ground has been harrowed, and the lumps not yet broken are brought to the surface, the roller is put on to crush and smooth them out. It is also very beneficial on light land, in dry weather, to help the land to

FIRST STAGES. 35

retain a sufficient quantity of moisture. I have found the use of a good horse roller to be of great advantage, both in breaking up and pulverizing lumpy land, and in firming down soil that has been thrown up very lightly during previous preparation. Such soil, until again compacted, is prone to become excessively dry; a result which is obviated by use of the roller. The top should be perfectly dry before rolling, in order to obtain the desired effect.

We have already alluded to subsoiling, and wish to remark here that the subsoil plough is a valuable, indeed, an indispensably necessary implement, and should be invariably put to use in the preparation of the ground for all root crops. The subsoil should follow after the land-side plough, in the same furrow, and go down to a depth of fifteen or eighteen inches. It usually takes two horses, as the larger sizes of ploughs do; and it is even harder for the team than common ploughing. There are small subsoilers which can be used with one horse; but if the land requires subsoiling at all, it is better economy to use the larger size and do the work more thoroughly.

In the concluding chapter, relating to Farm Implements, a sufficient description will be given of the different ploughs that are likely to be required, both landside and subsoil. At this point I wish to call attention to the great importance of keeping them always clean and bright. Never allow the ploughman to put his plough away with any dirt upon it. It is the sure mark of a poor ploughman, when his plough is covered with dirt, and goes through the land like a stick.

In fact, there are but very few good ploughmen to be had, and any employer is fortunate if he gets one. Many men will call themselves good at ploughing; but the men who really understand it, and do it as it should be done, are very scarce. When such a man is found, he should be kept on the place, if possible.

In ploughing land for the different crops, some plough about the same depth for everything; but the depth ought to be varied so as to suit the crop. For instance: all root crops should be ploughed from ten to twelve inches; while, for vine crops, six inches would be quite sufficient. Many take, in all cases, all they can to the furrow, making it, say, twelve or fourteen inches wide; but where the land is ploughed twelve inches deep, and a coat of manure is turned under at the same time, eight inches is wide enough to turn the furrow. In a "first-time" ploughing, of six inches deep, with no manure to turn under, twelve or fourteen inches may be taken at each furrow. Always plough all the land once in the fall and twice in the spring, but never when it is wet. Soil that is worked when very wet, except sometimes a very sandy piece, will scarcely recover from it for a whole season.

The purpose of the fall ploughing will be most completely accomplished by leaving the land in clods and rough, loose ridges, for the frost to operate upon during the winter. The greater the surface thus exposed to the influence of the atmosphere and changes of weather, the better for the soil and the coming season's crops. Moreover, late turning over the ground is an effectual means of killing off the larvæ of the May beetle, the pestilent white grub, and other larvæ of insects. Being disturbed from their winter quarters, they are to a great extent destroyed by exposure to the cold and air.

In the case of sod land to be prepared for tilled crops, there is a manifest advantage in turning it earlier in the season, so as to hasten the decay of the turf; but with land already under cultivation the case is entirely different, and the later it can be done the better.

It is, of course, assumed that everything necessary to a perfect drainage has been done prior to the process of preparation here described. Wherever the water has been extracted by drainage, it leaves a moderate moisture in the soil (until withdrawn by evaporation or taken up by the crop), which is exactly the condition most favorable to vegetation. The various processes of preparation, and later cultivation, are directed more especially to the maintenance of this condition.

The ground should be finely pulverized both at and below the surface, encouraging the roots to strike downwards and below the immediate influence of the hot sun. The air entering through the fine interstices of the soil condenses its latent moisture upon the cooler portions beneath the surface; thus contributing materially to the desired moisture, and also aiding the chemical changes attendant upon plant growth.

Another very important result of thorough and deep pulverization is the capacity afforded to the soil of directly absorbing and holding rain-water which otherwise would flow off wastefully, if not destructively, on the surface. Any one can see for himself the contrast between a soil which has received this thorough tilth, and one which has not; the latter looks well enough early in the season, but is burned up when the summer heats begin; while the deep-tilled land, on the contrary, holds the moisture like a damp sponge, down below the reach of the sun; and its presence there is plainly visible in the crop.

LAYING OUT LAND FOR CROPS.

A careful and definite plan, to be adhered to with as much strictness· as the nature of the case will admit, is essentially necessary at the very outset of operations. If one is well acquainted with the land he is cultivating, and knows what crops have been grown on each portion of it the previous season, of course he can make his plans accordingly. But if it be the first season of his occupation his arrangements must of necessity be guided by such information as he has. In that case, they will be partly experimental, and changes will be from time to time inevitably incurred; but this disadvantage should be avoided as far as careful attention to the subject will enable him.

It is a good idea, when practicable, to have a plan of the garden on paper, and to have this made during the winter; so that the intended arrangement of crops can be mapped out for the coming season. This will, of course, be a convenient guide in placing the manure for each crop at the point where it is to be used, in procuring supplies of seed, and also in many other details.

In mapping out a field in this manner, a person must

of course understand the rotation, or succession, of crops, in order to do the mapping intelligently; and accordingly we shall proceed to consider this subject next in order.

ROTATION OF CROPS.

The right succession of crops for enabling the cultivator to obtain paying results, both in the harvests to be gathered first and in condition of the soil for further culture, has always been a subject of much importance to every tiller of the soil; and is also interesting from a scientific point of view.

The difference between the old style of summer fallowing and the present well understood plans of rotation is so considerable that the two ways are styled by some the "old" and "new" agricultures.

Under the old system, an occasional year of fallowing was relied upon to rest the ground and renew the plant food in the soil, so that in the succeeding year a larger yield could be obtained than if the land had been cropped continuously.

Fallowing, although of benefit in some respects, is wasteful in two ways. The land of course is yielding no income in the idle year; here there is a loss of interest on capital. And then, too, as I am persuaded, there is always more or less waste and loss of plant food going on from any soil that is left exposed to the sun and rain during the summer months. At least two and often three crops in a year with constant tilth (including, with other benefits to the soil, the suppression of all weeds and wild growth) represent the "new" method. It is decidedly in contrast with the old at all points—and seems at all points to have the advantage of it.

The correct theory of rotation proposes, while making immediate use of the plant food already in the soil, at the same time to prepare the soil for producing the other crops that are next to follow. In arranging for a system of rotation, we should aim to grow such crops and under such culture as will keep the soil well supplied with humus, or plant food.

No exact rules can be laid down as to the order in which crops should be planted in rotation, but it should be remembered that some plants by nature feed near the surface (like corn, for instance), while others, take clover for an example, draw the most of their nourishment from deep down in the soil.

The object should be always to avoid following one deep-rooted crop by a similar one; taking great care to alternate them with others as constantly as possible. It is well, when practicable, to follow a slow-growing crop with one of quick growth, or *vice versa*. No root crop should follow one of a similar character; nor should vines follow vines. Alternation is always beneficial. Onions are very generally regarded as an exception to this general rule, and to some extent they doubtless are so; but I have not found it advisable to grow them on the same ground many consecutive years, as they are far more likely to become maggoty, and otherwise diseased, than when the ground is changed once in two or three seasons.

There is considerable truth in the suggestion that a good rotation can only be had when conducted by competent management, as hinted in the following extract from Wilmer Atkinson: "The rotation that is wanted is the one that will rotate most fertility into the farm and most cash into the pocket. Differing soils, differing advantages or disadvantages of markets, differing degrees of knowledge and experience in the growing and handling of certain crops are among the many elements that enter into the question. In any case, it must be the one that will yield the largest amount of sale product, with which to meet current expenses of business and living, and at the same time store increase of fertility in the land for future use."

Just what this is appears to him a doubtful question, quite too intricate to be discussed, and on which it would be quite impracticable for one farmer to advise another. On the contrary, we hold that accumulated experience has settled many points in a way not likely to be reversed, and affords much valuable aid in promoting the objects on which all are agreed, viz.: immediate cash returns and future productiveness of the soil.

The subject of the judicious succession of crops will be repeatedly reverted to, and illustrated by many practical examples, fully explained. These will be found in the cultural directions which accompany our descriptions of the different vegetables, hereafter given in this book.

Manures and Fertilizers.

The provision, preparation, and use of manures and fertilizers is one of the most important and diversified subjects in the whole business of market gardening; and to cover these points advantageously and economically involves a very considerable amount both of thought and labor.

In my own practice, the dressing that is usually supplied per acre for growing the two or three crops which it is customary to obtain each year from garden land consists of from twenty to twenty-five cords of well decomposed stable manure, put on broadcast.

The manner of applying depends somewhat on the crop; and many special instructions will be given in the cultural directions which are furnished with our descriptions of various vegetables. In general, however, the manure is either spread in advance of the first ploughing, and then turned under, or is put on after the ground has been worked once, being then worked in with the second ploughing. The distribution of the manure is generally by the use of tip-carts, as there is no spreader now in use that will put on twenty cords per acre by once going over.

During the summer, fall, and winter, manure for the succeeding season is hauled out from the city. The sources of supply are the large stables, from which the accumulations of manure must be removed at brief intervals all through the year. It is usually piled in some place near where it is to be used. However, during the summer, it is my usual practice to put it into my cellars, and there let the hogs work it over until fall. This manure, so prepared, is, in my judgment, the best I have, and is used for growing cabbages as well as other vegetables; although many people do not consider hog manure desirable for that crop.

In the beginning of the winter this is teamed out upon the fields where it is to be used; the cellar is then filled again, and its contents remain in it until spring. All the manure which is drawn from the city in the summer and fall is overhauled in the early winter, and is again worked over in the spring before applying it to the land. It will then be quite fine, and fitted for nourishing any kind of crop.

In distributing the manure, to put on twenty-five cords to the acre, reckoning four tip-cart loads to the cord, requires one hundred loads; making three piles to the load, we shall have piles twelve feet apart each way. In applying twenty cords to the acre, still reckoning four tip-cart loads to the cord and three piles to the load, we shall have piles twelve by fifteen feet apart. In applying fifteen cords to the acre, with loads and piles as before, we shall have piles sixteen by fifteen feet apart.

This last named amount is one which is seldom used in a market garden, except where one crop is to occupy the ground through the whole season. Where two crops are to be grown with one application of manure, the second amount is the one to be used; and where three are to be grown, use the first named amount.

It is very wasteful to expose manure unnecessarily to sun and wind. Never spread manure one day to be ploughed in the next.

It may not be amiss to mention, lest its importance should be overlooked or under-estimated, the great advantage of taking care, in spreading the manure, to do it evenly, and so that the heaps shall not be made to overlap. One heap is then made to join up to another, and the whole ground fares alike as regards the supply of manure. This seems obvious enough, and practical works on farming already have sought to enforce this view. But as we read in one recently published, "there is more in this point than is generally supposed by farmers, who, in many cases, are careless and wasteful in this respect, giving too much in some places and too little in others. The consequence is uneven growth over the different parts of the field; perhaps rank in some places, and in others a half-starved crop."

The same writer suggests another important point in spreading, which is to break up the lumps and scatter the manure about in a fine state; unless this is done the field cannot be evenly fertilized. There is work about this, and some hired men will neglect and avoid it if they are permitted, but it should not only be insisted upon, but looked after, and its faithful performance insured. Solid manure should never be allowed to ferment, either out-doors or under a cover, without the presence of absorbent material to take up the gases evolved during the process. This is the basis upon which the whole theory of composts and management of the compost heaps is admitted to rest.

As already implied, it is necessary for green manure to undergo fermentation, in order to make its constituent elements available as plant food. Some good gardeners insist that all manure should be thoroughly fined before it goes upon the land; that none should be carried on that is not as fine as the soil upon which it is to be spread. It is undoubtedly advantageous to conform to this rule as far as is reasonably possible. However, green manure may be applied in the fall and covered in with the fall ploughing, in which case the fermentation, when it occurs, takes place within the soil, making it mellow and rich. At this stage, and until the warm weather of the following spring induces fermentation, there can be no waste of the manure by soakage of water, because it is still insoluble.

The case is different with fine compost, or with the ordinary pulverized commercial fertilizers, the benefit from which must be secured in a crop taken the same season or it may never be obtained.

In case three crops are to be grown and the third crop is to be cabbage or celery, the application of about one half ton of some good commercial fertilizer to each acre would be very beneficial. It should be put on when the third crop has made about half its growth. In many similar cases, guano, superphosphate, bone-dust, and the like may be used in combination with the stable manure already in the soil, with excellent results.

This use of commercial fertilizers in connection with stable manure has become quite common with market gardeners during the past few years. Some people even have an idea that, by the use of commercial fertilizers and without any other manuring, land can be kept in a proper state of fertility and condition to grow crops, year after year. Possibly this might at times be done, on some soils, and where only one crop each year was to be produced; but in the market gardens where are grown several crops in a single season, maintaining a constant drain upon the nourishment afforded by the soil, such a plan would not be found to work well.

One reason for this is, that where two or three crops are to be grown during the season, the particular kind of fertilizer which would be required by one crop might be of little or no value to the others. And moreover, it would be a very difficult matter to apply, from time to time, sufficient quantities of commercial fertilizers to carry all the crops to maturity. But stable manure answers well for all crops, and so, if desired (though not always necessary or convenient), enough can be applied at the time of ploughing, in the spring, to carry all the crops through the season.

Green or composted stable manure, besides the increased store of plant food it directly provides for the growing crop, increasing its vigor, and enabling it to strike deeper, has no doubt a beneficial effect upon the mechanical condition or texture of the soil. This is not the case with the commercial fertilizers, which, if used without the stable manure as a corrective, in course of time make the land sodden and heavy. Thus it will be seen that, for various reasons, commercial fertilizers cannot wholly or even largely take the place of stable manure, while they are nevertheless much esteemed for use in combination with it. Since the use of commercial fertilizers has become general the price of stable manure has decreased; and while the convenience of procuring the former makes them more particularly convenient and valuable to the stock-feeding farmers (who are generally remote from the city), their introduction has also been of much benefit to the gardeners near the large cities, in thus reducing the cost of stable manure. The price would be even lower than it is, were it not for the fact that large quantities are now shipped by the car-load from the cities to distant points, while but a few years ago no instance of the kind had ever occurred.

The old-fashioned privy-vault or cesspool is a source of supply once largely depended upon, but now only rarely met with; as the general extension of water-works to all the more compact centres of population, and even to isolated country houses, has caused a discontinuance of the earlier practice of allowing night-soil to accumulate, and depending upon intermittent removal by carts.

Still there is sometimes a case of this kind to be dealt with. The owner of the premises, if he has facilities, will generally prefer to compost his material on the spot, with a liberal proportion of light, dry loam, rendering it perfectly inoffensive. It is a highly stimulating fertilizer, and may be productive of excellent results if discreetly used. When the owner's object is simply to get rid of the contents of his vault, — although formerly this was accomplished by bailing into wagons specially built for the work (similar to the offal-wagons now used for collecting kitchen refuse) — it is found more convenient to use an ordinary (tight built) cart or wagon; in this, earth, chopped straw, ashes, street sweepings, or any other convenient absorbents are conveyed to the spot. With earth and ashes a basin-shaped receptacle is formed on the ground adjacent to the cesspool, keeping a reserve at hand of absorbent material to be added by degrees as the work progresses. The vault is then bailed out into the space so provided, and, its contents being mixed with a due proportion of absorbents, and, finally, the earth around the edges being worked in, the whole mass is then ready to be loaded and transported.

By this method the material is made convenient to handle, and as little disagreeable as ordinary manure from the barnyard. In England, and on the Continent, by the use of long straw, judiciously disposed during the loading, the mixed material above described is built up into a stack reaching two or three feet high, above the sides of the wagon or cart, and so great loads of it are carried many miles without loss. The straw is spread so that half of its length projects over the sides or ends of the load, and in layers—the inner ends of the straw being covered and held fast by the alternate layers of compost—and the outer ends are then bent upwards and backwards, and similarly confined. Racks for sides and ends are convenient but when the load is carefully put together may be dispensed with.

Wood ashes, where they can be obtained, form one of the best of fertilizers, and when unleached are generally richer in potash (which is one of the most important elements) than most commercial fertilizers. From the fact that ashes are almost entirely lacking in nitrogen, it is not advisable to rely on them alone and continuously, year after year; but if applied about once in three years, with stable manure put on in the meantime, they will be found of great value. For cabbage and onions, which require a very large amount of potash, ashes are especially suitable.

For manuring in the hill, which is in many cases highly advantageous, it is ordinarily preferred to use guano, superphosphates, and the like, because of the facility with which they can be put in; care being always taken to stir them in well, so that the sprouting seeds shall escape absolute contact with the unmixed fertilizer—which would be destructive.

Good, ripe, well-worked compost is also employed; often made from materials specially purchased to mix up (like fish compost, made where fish-waste is readily procurable), but also produced, under judicious management, from every thing in the shape of decomposable material that can be gathered up about the place. And if due attention is given to collecting together all waste material — litter, leaves, weeds, and the like — and stacking them in alternate layers with fresh loam, or road-scrapings, the result will be a handsome lot of uniform, fine compost. It should always be built up in layers, each layer spread out so as to cover the preceding layer uniformly; which will secure compost of even quality. It should be protected from washing or leaching by a rough covering of boards, so placed as to shed the rains.

Occasional layers of fresh dung, doses of lime and ashes, and drenching the mass from time to time with liquid manure, will enable the proper fermentation.

There are innumerable ways of increasing the bulk and enhancing the quality of the compost heap, which can best be mastered by the study of any good manual on the subject; and we do not aim here at superseding any of these treatises. Our object is mainly to call attention to this means of utilizing all manner of decomposable trash, and converting it into valuable plant food. There is an old saying, that "anything that grows in one summer will decay before the next;" and this hint may be profitable as a guide in collecting vegetable matter for the compost heap.

The presence of the loam, or loamy mixtures, in the heap is quite important. It has been said that where sods, muck and weeds form a part of the mass, it is not alone the vegetable matter which has been brought in that constitutes a material addition; perhaps it is not even the principal one. There is always considerable earth adhering. "The fermentation, induced by the dung and liquid manure and the action of the lime or ashes added, works upon the *earth* adhering to the roots and forming a considerable part both of sods and muck; and develops an admirable quality of plant food." Hence this element of the compost heap, which is generally overlooked as unimportant, should never be wanting — instead of diluting, it in reality reinforces the other manurial elements.

Liquid manure is seldom at hand in large quantities, and not much advance has been made in using it directly upon the land under crop. When this is done, it should be in a very diluted state. Even if so much diluted that it seems to run perfectly clear, it may still be found sufficiently strong; if too strong its use would be injurious rather than helpful, and might often destroy a crop entirely. There is far more danger of getting it too strong than of making it too weak. It may be doubted, indeed, whether the diluting element, water, is not, at least, an equal cause of the fertility which sometimes attends its use, when directly applied. The result either of watering or liquid manuring will be less favorable in a cool season than in a hot one; owing to the reduction of temperature occasioned by wet applications to the soil.

A way of procuring liquid manure — convenient when a small quantity only is required — is to leach solid stable manure as ashes are leached for obtaining lye. For special results, solutions of specific commercial fertilizers are valuable, and are easily made. For instance, liquid nitrate of soda is obtained by dissolving one pound of the nitrate in twelve gallons of water. It is beneficial to all garden crops, though particularly recommended for grass plats — but its chief value to the vegetable grower is as a destroyer of slugs and other garden pests.

The most valuable liquid manure is, however, the urine of stabled animals, which when not allowed to run to waste is ordinarily taken up by absorbents kept under the animals, in the stalls or in the cellar beneath them. Sometimes, however, it is conducted by natural flow in gutters and pipes to a tank from which it may be pumped. It is very valuable, more so than the solid excrement from the same animals; and more effectual means of saving and applying it than those now generally practised will doubtless soon come into use. In applying it directly to the soil amongst growing plants it requires, as already said, to be greatly diluted. Small amounts pumped at intervals over the compost heap promote fermentation.

In purchasing manure, preference should be given to that of grain-fed animals. The value of all animal excrement depends more on the character of the food consumed than on the kind of animal. But it is convenient to know the average composition of the solid droppings of different animals, and the following data have once been published in the *Gardener's Monthly*. The excrement standing highest in value is *sheep dung* (this not being obtainable in our vicinity, we give its analysis merely for comparison). It contains in 100 parts, of water, 68.71; azotized matter, 23.16; saline, 8.13. Horse manure consists of water, 75.31; *geine*, or organic matter, 20.67; salts, 4.02. (The geine is composed of — carbon, 9.56; hydrogen, 1.26; oxygen, 9.31; and nitrogen 0.54.) Cow manure contains, geine, 15.45; salts, 0.95; water, 83.60. Contrary to the general idea, that of the horse outranks that of the cow.

The list of materials available to the gardener and cultivator for enriching the soil comprises the following principal items: the animal manures (like those whose analysis has been given), fish, bones of animals, lime, gypsum, wood ashes, common salt, soot, peat-earth, seaweeds, malt dust, rape-cake and linseed-cake, green succulent plants, and commercial fertilizers.

Much has recently been added to the stock of general information on the nature and action of manures.

All the more the subject is one which demands constant study and reflection on the part of the practical cultivator. In view of the great variety of conditions presenting themselves, it often seems next to impossible for him to select from the mass of available matter the points likely to be of assistance to him. Yet by diligent reading, and carefully discriminating what he reads, he will soon begin to feel the benefit of combining the experience of others with that which he gains for himself, and will find that the former is by far the less costly of the two. On this general topic of manures, many well written works may be found in most libraries. We recommend for reading, once and again, till its contents become thoroughly familiar, Harris' "Talks on Manures," published a number of years ago. Its style is varied and interesting, and the matter is highly instructive. Every farmer should use this, or some equivalent book, as a constant reference and guide in providing and applying manures; and there is no other book that we know of which presents this subject so clearly and intelligibly, and at the same time in such an interesting manner—almost every page is as readable as a story.

APPLICATION OF MANURES.

Further general suggestions on this subject might seem to some almost unnecessary, but, nevertheless, this is an important part of market-garden work, and well worthy of attentive study. As garden crops, to be of marketable quality, require to be grown quickly, it is plainly requisite that the land be brought into the best possible condition to begin with, and then that the artificial fertilizers or further manurings, whatever they may be, should be applied in such a way that the growing crops can readily reach and take up this supplementary nourishment.

In what has been said on Preparation of the Soil, we have included many detailed directions for applying manures to the soil, and amongst them have recommended having the land ploughed once in advance of the first application of the manure. This gives a chance for the manure (especially if it is a little coarse) to be worked into the soil more thoroughly by the second ploughing than it otherwise would. However, except in comparatively few instances, the presence of coarse manure is a serious impediment and disadvantage in the process of cultivation. It should be in a fine state, reduced to this condition by slowly conducted previous fermentation, and should be very thoroughly intermixed with the soil.

Of course, as already said, it is very important that market-garden crops be grown quickly, and right here is the reason why quick-growing crops require more manure than others that take a whole season to complete their growth: it is because the latter have more time in which to feel about and collect their necessary nourishment from the soil and atmosphere; but the former must have their food in abundance, and it must be placed within easy reach of the feeding roots, or there will be a most decided shortage in the result.

There are great differences in the requirements of the various crops, and no set rule can be given that will be adapted for regulating the quantity of manure to be applied to all crops and on all soils. Some specific instructions for special cases appear in the following pages.

Where but one crop per year is to be taken from land which is already in fairly good condition, ten or twelve cords per acre of well decomposed manure would be considered, ordinarily, as a sufficient supply; but on land to be double-cropped, twenty cords would be none too much. This should be ploughed in lightly, so as to be left lying near the surface.

If the first ploughing should be done in the fall, the manure can be applied then, and remain lying out on the surface until spring, as it does not lose by so doing. During a dry season, unless the land can be properly irrigated or watered, a crop will manifestly be unable to draw the proper amount of nourishment from the soil, since all plant food of every description has to be not merely in a soluble form but actually in solution before it can be taken up and assimilated by the plants. For this reason it is now felt necessary, in view of the continually recurring droughts, to provide effectual means of irrigation.

Sometimes, however, a crop comes to a stand-still by reason of having exhausted all the fertilizing matter contained in the soil, of a sort available to its requirements; and in such instances the trained eye of the practical gardener can usually detect what is lacking for the crop; and he may supply the need by an application of some specific commercial fertilizer. It would be difficult to explain to a wholly unexperienced person just how to detect the wants of the crops, but a little acquaintance with their normal habits of growth will speedily teach one what he needs to observe.

It is imperative, even in an economical view, where a crop is checked in growth from want of fertilizing matter, that some quick-acting fertilizer be promptly applied, for upon the question of a few dollars' expenditure at this crisis may depend all the difference between a crop and no crop. Whenever the need of such an application occurs, it is better to sow the fertilizer broadcast than to place it directly on the hill and about the plant; and the labor of applying it is less. Liquid manure may be applied by the process already described for irrigating, in a furrow opened about a foot from the row; more or less, according to the growth the plants have made.

CHAPTER III.

SELECTION OF SEEDS — THEIR VITALITY — SEED-GROWING — SOWING THE SEED — CULTIVATION OF CROPS — CONSTRUCTION AND CARE OF HOT-BEDS — GARDENING IN HOT-HOUSES — GATHERING THE CROPS — CAPITAL AND LABOR INVOLVED.

PERHAPS we might truthfully say that the most important of all points in gardening is the right selection of seeds; for without good seed the care and expense devoted to selecting and fitting the land, or procuring and using implements, fertilizers, etc., is all bestowed in vain.

By good seed, we not only mean such as will germinate properly, but such as is true to name, and of the very best selected strains. And it is proper in this connection to say that no one need expect to get seed such as we have spoken of at such absurdly low prices as much cheap stuff is sold for. Better to pay twice the market price for an article that is first-class in every respect than have poor trash, even if to be had as a gift.

Always look for quality first; and when satisfied in this respect pay the price, if it is anywise reasonable; for you must remember that these extra strains have cost an amount of labor and expense in growing them largely beyond that required by common-grown stock.

Of course, as we have already said, it is always important, and in some degree essential, that none but the best seed be used ; but with some crops this is most especially necessary, and a neglect will result in the most disastrous kind of a failure. Take, for instance, either cabbage, cauliflower, or celery. These are vegetables with regard to which the greatest care has to be exercised, to procure the proper kind of seed stock. Also with onions, lettuce, and cucumbers this is no less important.

It may be well to add, while on this point, that there is more than one advantage in purchasing your seed supply early in the season, and before the spring rush comes on. By so doing you are enabled to get the best that there is in stock, as the supplies have not then been greatly drawn upon ; and by attending to the matter before every one is driven with orders you have a better chance to make your selections, and of avoiding mistakes.

It is quite important, unless you can rely absolutely upon the dealer from whom you purchase, to employ some means of testing the quality of seeds. Some have recommended as the speediest way, though not altogether a sure one, putting a few on top of a hot stove ; such as are good will crack like corn in parching ; the bad will burn without noise and with very little motion. A more reliable way is to place a little cotton-wool or moss in a tumbler containing water, and let it stand in a warm room while the experiment is in progress. Place the seeds to be tested on the wool or moss so arranged, and they will germinate sooner than they would in ordinary planting. The proportion of bad seed — that is, of seed which has lost its vitality — will be recognized in this way; but as regards the quality of the strain and whether they are true to name, there can be no proof or guarantee in advance of the crop they bring, except procuring them from a dealer who is recognized as reliable, and who knows, himself, what he is selling.

VITALITY OF SEEDS.

As regards the period for which seeds may be kept without destroying or seriously impairing their vitality, this varies with different seeds. Opinion varies also as to the time which may be assigned as the limit in the case of each separate kind. It is ordinarily thought, and perhaps it is safest to hold as a general rule, that the seeds which mature in one season are the best for next year's planting. However, seeds of good original vitality may be expected to germinate freely, if properly cared for, at periods after maturity not greater than shown in the table on the following page.

We have to remark here that the duration of the germinating power of seeds depends very materially upon the circumstances under which they have been harvested and kept. Nothing has a greater tendency to destroy it than the influence of dampness and heat; owing to which causes it often occurs that good seed, purchased from dealers in whom reliance can be placed, and kept not a great while on hand, fails to come up. Thus far no better method is known for keeping seeds in good condition till wanted than putting them in linen bags and storing in a dry, moderately cool, and well ventilated place.

Any seeds, of which the germinating power continues active for five years, on an average, do not entirely lose it after the lapse of ten years or more. In this class are included most of the seeds sown in the market garden — those which possess a less degree of vitality are Corn, Dandelion, Leek, Onion, Okra, Peas, Parsnip, Parsley, Radish, Salsify, and Spinach.

LENGTHS OF TIME FOR WHICH DIFFERENT SEEDS RETAIN THEIR VITALITY.

Artichoke	5 years.	Kohl-rabi	7	years.
Asparagus	4 "	Leek	2	"
Beans	5 "	Lettuce	5	"
Beets	5 "	Melon	7	"
Broccoli	5 "	Onion	2	"
Brussels Sprouts,	7 "	Okra	3	"
Cabbage	7 "	Peas	4	"
Carrot	5 "	Parsnip	1	"
Cauliflower	7 "	Pumpkin	7	"
Celery	8 "	Parsley	3	"
Corn	2 "	Radish	3	"
Cucumber	12 "	Salsify	2	"
Dandelion	3 "	Spinach	3	"
Egg-plant	7 "	Squash	7	"
Endive	9 "	Tomato	5	"
Kale	5 "	Turnip	5	"

The general rule above suggested, giving preference to last year's seed, has some exceptions. Plants such as melons, cucumbers, and squashes (though they grow vines most vigorously from fresh seeds) are thought to set and mature their fruit better when grown from that which is older. Beans are included by some in the same category.

SEED GROWING.

Every one who makes market gardening a business is obliged to raise at least a portion of the seed which he plants; and in order to do this successfully, as regards its vigor and productiveness, and so as to obtain the choicest of each kind, great pains must be taken in the selection and care of the seed stocks.

In selecting the stocks from which the seed is to be saved, the very best of the season should always be taken. Particular rows, or even individual plants in different parts of the field, must be marked and reserved for the purpose; and although this is very expensive and tedious it is the only safe and satisfactory way. By so doing the stock is constantly improving year by year; while, if the product of the whole field is saved for seed, as is done by many seed growers, there must be more or less deterioration.

Owing to the differences in climate, some kinds of seeds can be grown to much better advantage in localities other than our own; and, although most of the seeds which are planted in our market gardens can be grown successfully in America, there are a few among these which can be raised to far better advantage in foreign countries. No doubt, one reason for this is that these countries enjoy a climate much more equable than ours — a condition which is more favorable for all crops, and renders the results of cultivation much more reliable.

The cauliflower, in particular, has a seed which cannot be grown with any certainty in this country; while foreign growers are almost as certain of a crop as we are with cabbage.

Although, in the case of many of the seeds which are produced by market gardeners, through careful selection, in the manner described, one could often purchase his supply from dealers for one-half what it costs him to produce it himself, the quality of his own selected stock may be more than enough better to make up the difference in cost. I have raised vegetables in such large quantities that I have been induced to grow my own seed, to a great extent, and, having often had a surplus, have supplied my neighbors; and my trade in seeds, commencing in this way, has constantly increased from the beginning, until I have been finally obliged to open a seed store in the city, for the convenience of my many customers.

Of course, I do not by any means profess to grow all the seeds I catalogue; but there are several kinds which I can and do grow very successfully, and which I have, by years of careful selection, greatly improved. Of these seeds I grow all that I sell; and, in order to distinguish them from the common strains, I have designated them as "Arlington-grown" seeds. I do not profess to sell these seeds at any such low prices as seeds of the same varieties can often be bought for, elsewhere, from dealers who buy up their stock here and there, of any one from whom they can purchase cheapest. Any one who will give the matter a moment's thought will see that I cannot compete in price with these cheap grades of seeds.

It is a false view of economy that leads any one to purchase cheap seed, — for a few dollars saved in the beginning may make a shortage of one-half, or more, in the crop. I have always made it a practice when purchasing seed for my own use (of such varieties as I do not raise, and so have been obliged to buy), to secure the *best, regardless of cost,* and have always found this to pay. Quality, not price, is the chief point to look to in purchasing seed.

The same rule applies to the case of the seed-grower producing seeds either for his own use or for sale — the expense of the process must be disregarded, and the excellence of the product made the prime consideration. All seeds should be gathered as soon as they mature — for exposure to the weather is injurious to their power of vegetating when planted. They should be dried in the shade, and in a warm place, but not where they will be affected by the direct heat of the fire.

SOWING THE SEED.

In the preparatory stages of the work of raising a crop, all the points we have included above are of vital importance and need close attention. The successful germination of the seed, no matter how carefully the sowing may be done, must depend largely upon the condition of the ground. But, on the other hand, it is no less true that, unless the seed is carefully and judiciously placed in the ground, and properly covered, the crop cannot get a good start, no matter how well the land has been prepared or how good the seed is.

It is far better, when possible, to put seed into freshly prepared soil, as it is sure to get a better start than on land which has been turned over long enough to have become crusty and lumpy on the surface. Again, it is preferable, when possible, to sow seed immediately after a rain rather than just before it comes; since, in the case of the finer seeds, more especially, the crust which begins to form on all garden soils immediately after a rain will partly shut out the air and will tend to prevent free germination. Where one encounters the misfortune of a heavy fall of rain occurring just after the planting of a field or bed, it will be well to go over the ground with rakes, and break the crust; and such treatment may make a difference of fifty per cent. in the stand obtained.

With seed having a thick husk, like squash, cucumber, or melon, it is obviously of peculiar importance that the soil be in just the right condition — in order to be sure that sufficient moisture and air may reach the seed — much more than with thin-husked kinds that germinate quickly, like cabbage, turnip, and radish; but, still, even these finer seeds need the most vigilant attention and the utmost care that can be given in sowing them, to secure the best results.

In sowing the seed of beets, squashes, and parsnips, and also peas, beans, and all similar seeds, it is necessary also to plant deeper than the finer seeds, from the fact that the husk is thicker, and it requires more moisture to cause germination.

Most of the finer seeds are sown by machine, at different distances apart, and likewise at different depths, varying, according to the kind, from one-fourth of an inch to one inch; being governed partly by the size of the seed, and also by the season of the year. Seed put in during the hot, dry weather of summer must, for obvious reasons, be covered a little deeper than early in spring, when the ground is moist enough for their speedy germination, even if very near the surface.

CULTIVATION OF CROPS.

After the seed that we have sown has come up, the frequent stirring of the soil will prove beneficial. It is not generally necessary to caution any one against stirring the soil too frequently, still this may, not impossibly, be sometimes overdone, at least as regarded from a financial point of view.

Following a rain, and after the land is dried sufficiently to be in good working condition, is the best possible time for giving the soil a thorough stirring; for then it will be left in a fresh, lively condition, that will give the growing crop a surprising start.

It may be well to note here that it is not profitable to stir the soil when it is too wet, or to hoe crops when they are dripping with water, as some people do; even cabbages, celery, and turnips are not benefited, if indeed they escape serious injury, under such treatment.

In cultivating crops of any description, it is necessary to bear in mind that, when they are young and growing rapidly, it will be proper to cultivate deeper and nearer to the plants than at a later stage, when growth is not so rapid. At the later stage, such active cultivation would have a tendency to ripen off the crop, rather than promote its growth.

During a dry season, or a period of extended drought, the more frequently the soil is stirred around a growing crop the better; as the loosening up of the surface soil will draw the moisture from below upwards, within reach of the feeding roots of the plants, and thus enable them to absorb it.

In the case of any crop planted in rows, it is a good plan to stir the soil and cut down the weeds, immediately after the plants come up, in the following manner: Take an ordinary **A** harrow and remove the front tooth; then drive along each row of plants, keeping it exactly between the horses and central to the harrow. This harrowing will not disturb them in the least, and just at this stage will promote their growth surprisingly. The weeds of course will not be exterminated entirely, but their first early growth will be effectually destroyed, and they will more easily be kept under during the rest of the season.

Parasitic insects and vegetable parasites (to which latter class belong smut, blight, mildew, etc.) cause heavy losses and disappointments to all cultivators of the land both on farms and in gardens. The more thrifty the habit and condition of the plants, the less will they be liable to such ravages. Thorough and constant cultivation disturbs and destroys the larvæ, reinforces the plant, and enables it to withstand parasitic attacks, both animal and vegetable, to good advantage. Further suggestions on this topic scarcely belong to this chapter, but will be given later in the work.

CONSTRUCTION OF HOT-BEDS.

For a location, a spot facing the south, with a slope in that direction, is the most desirable. After the location has been selected, a fence should be erected six feet high, and of the length which the bed is to be, to serve as a protection from the wind, and as a support for mats and shutters. For convenience, the fence or wind-break should slant back a little from the bottom, — about one foot: it will then form a better support for mats and shutters when leaned against it, and will be much more convenient in working around the beds.

The first plank should be set about three and a half feet from the base of the fence, and should be two inches thick by twelve inches. The front plank should be two inches narrower. Place the back plank two and a half inches above the ground, and hold in place by driving stakes at the end and middle. Continue the planking in this manner until the desired length is reached. The stakes should, of course, be nailed to the planks. Place the front plank six feet from the first, and sink into the ground so that the upper edge will be five inches lower than the top of the first, which makes a slant of five inches to carry off the water. Continue this the same length as the first, and you will then have a bed six feet wide and of the desired length. Shovel out the loam sufficient to bank the planks on the outside about half the height, putting in spreaders to keep from crowding in. Let the ground freeze about three inches deep, then cover the banking with leaves or litter to keep out the frost.

Supplying the Heat.

If the bed is for lettuce, throw out the loam on the back side of the bed to the depth of twenty-four inches from the upper edge of the plank, and twenty-two inches in front, and of the length required, so as to make room for the manure. Prepare the required heat by selecting moderately coarse horse manure four or five days before using, turning it once or twice. A horse-cart load containing about thirty-six feet is sufficient for a bed six feet square, or for two sashes, the depth of the manure being one foot. This should be trodden down, and made smooth on top; then put in the loam from under the next two sashes, cover to the depth of eight inches, and continue in this manner as far as required; then bring the loam which was taken from the first two sashes, and put it under the last, which completes the bed.

For heating material, various articles are sometimes used, such as hop waste from the breweries, cotton waste, etc.; but where fresh horse manure can be obtained at anything like reasonable rates, it is far better, and, all things considered, is actually more economical; as the manure can, of course, be used on the land after it has served its purpose in the beds; and it is then, as ordinarily considered, worth half the original cost. Then, too, where manure is used the ammonia which escapes during the heating process is of great benefit to the growing crops, while from other material there is no such benefit — substantially nothing but the heat is derived. Steam has been applied to hotbeds, but with no good results as yet.

Radishes require less heat than lettuce, just as a crop of young cauliflower or cabbage requires less heat than tomatoes, egg-plants, or others of a tropical nature. For radishes, a cart-load of manure, containing thirty-six feet, would be sufficient for nine feet of bed, or three sashes, and should be covered by one foot of loam. For forcing cucumbers more heat is required than for lettuce according to the season. In any case, the bed should stand a day after it is prepared, to allow the soil to heat through; it is then ready for seeds or plants.

The quantity of heating material to be used will not however depend entirely upon the crop to be grown; we must also take into account the season of the year when it is to be started. With lettuce, for instance: if the crop were to be planted in December, a foot of fresh manure would be necessary; while in February or March one-half that quantity would be sufficient. But for such tropical-natured plants as tomatoes, cucumbers, or egg-plants, a foot of heating material would be none too much at any season.

A crop of radishes would not perhaps require quite as much heat as lettuce during the winter months; still it would need about the quantity stated to keep the bed properly warm. If started in March, no strong bottom heat would be required; and they will succeed well on second heat, such as is in a bed from which a crop of lettuce or other vegetables has just been removed. In this case the crop will often do better than when sown in a freshly made bed, as in the latter the ammonia, which new heating material always throws out, would have a tendency to drive the crop too much to tops; which is not what is wanted with root crops.

The continuous care of hot-beds after the crop has been started forms one of the most important branches of work in the market garden. The beds require to be covered and uncovered every day, and constant attendance and vigilance are necessary to maintain the proper temperature. The amount of heat to be aimed at, as we have already said, depends upon the crop.

Lettuce beds, during the winter months, should be be kept at a temperature ranging at from 50° to 70°. For radishes it may range from 40° to 60°; while for cucumbers and tomatoes it must range decidedly higher, say from 70° to 90°, or even 100°.

In the spring of the year, it is quite a serious task for a man to take charge of say 1,000 sashes, with a half a dozen different crops under them. He must of course have a thorough understanding of their requirements in respect to heat, moisture, and a variety of other conditions. He must be a person of considerable experience or he cannot be qualified to undertake the entire management of crops so cultivated. It will be found that much depends on their receiving the right care, and always just at the right time.

If the first crop is started in November or December, and the beds are properly handled, three and sometimes even four crops may be taken from the glass each season. In regard to the amount of produce that can be taken off, per sash, each season, of course much depends on skilful management; but if the beds are properly attended to (where three crops are grown) the results might, ordinarily, be expected to be about as follows: say for the first crop, $2.50; for the second, $2.00; and the third, $1.50; making a total of $6.00 per sash. These figures are of course often exceeded, and even doubled; but we are now giving estimates of a result as near an average as possible.

The first crop embraced in the foregoing estimate would be lettuce, four dozen to each sash, at 62 1-2c. per dozen. The next, either lettuce or radishes; the third, cucumbers, which would be put under the glass about the first of April and begin to bear June 1st. The latter crop varies in price according to the season, some years averaging as high as three dollars per sash; but for a large quantity, a cash return amounting to a dollar and a half per sash would be considered by most growers as reasonably good.

Gardening in Hot-Houses.

Forty years ago very little growing was done under glass; and if any one had as many as one hundred sash he was considered quite an extensive market gardener. But when early vegetables began to be grown in the South and sent into our market, some twenty years ago, our gardeners began to increase their use of sash; and some ten years ago hot-houses were put into service. These have gradually become more and more relied upon in the growing of plants and vegetables, until now a market gardener who has no hot-house is considered far behind the times. There are even now many thousands of sashes used every spring for covering hot beds; but the houses are much easier of management, and with the use of either steam heat or hot water pipes nearly all the kinds of vegetables that can be forced are grown in houses.

There are many advantages secured by this method of culture. We can employ our men the whole season and are thereby enabled to procure better help; and we have something to carry to market the whole season through. Besides, the houses are a great help in running the sash, as the plants can all be started in the houses and transplanted, no matter what the weather may happen to be.

One must have considerable intelligence and skill to run a number of houses together with several thousand sash; and a market gardener of to-day must understand many different matters. He must be an engineer, a machinist, a carpenter, a chemist, a botanist and a horticulturist. It will cost him time and study to make himself familiar with all he has to look after. It will take him all of five years' time, and he must show himself an able scholar, even then.

In hot-houses the temperature required being attained by the use of pipes conveying steam or hot water, relatively a small amount of manure will be requisite as compared with that required to create and maintain heat, in beds, by the process of fermentation.

It requires a fifty-horse-power boiler to heat one hundred thousand cubic feet of space to a tempera-

Interior of one of W. W. Rawson's Hot-Houses at Arlington, Mass. Occupied with Lettuce: 24,000 Plants growing, and to mature, together

ture of 60° when the outside air is at zero Fahrenheit. It takes one ton of coal for every five hundred cubic feet of space to heat at same temperature and carry through the season from November 1 to the first of May, and there must be provided one foot in length of one and a quarter-inch steam pipe for every twenty cubic feet of space to heat the pipes to be equally distributed. With the use of hot water, instead of steam, it takes a four-inch pipe to do the same amount of heating that is done by the one and a quarter-inch steam pipe; and if the weather comes off warm in the morning the pipes of hot water will remain hot; while steam heat can be immediately shut off and can be let on again at any moment. With water it takes from one to two hours to get the pipes warm again after being cooled off.*

GATHERING THE CROPS.

In market gardening the term "harvest" cannot be applied as it was in olden times to the gathering of the grain and other crops in the fall of the year. Under modern usages there is no real season of harvesting, but, on the contrary, the "seed-time and harvest" seasons, both of them, extend the whole year round.

Much experience is required to enable one to know just when to harvest market-garden crops, and this does not always or solely depend on their stage of maturity. The market gardener of to-day would say that the time to harvest a crop is when it will bring the most money. Although, of course, there are some vegetables that cannot be gathered until they are ripe, as

* Consult Chapter VII.

otherwise they are practically worthless — such as melons, celery, and cauliflower, which it would be folly to touch until they had reached maturity — yet also there are some, like beets, lettuce, spinach, etc., which, after reaching a certain early stage of growth, can be marketed readily, and to profit.

In crops that are to be marketed when young and tender, it is plainly of vital importance to have experienced hands for the work, as such articles are very easily injured and rendered unsalable by careless handling and packing for transportation.

The same considerations, though perhaps less obvious, are equally important in the case of vegetables that are to be stored for the winter. These also should be harvested and handled with care, and placed in storage only when dry or in just the right condition, for their keeping qualities must largely depend on their treatment at this time.

Amounts of Capital and Labor Required.

Among gardeners, opinions vary as to the area that an individual may wisely include in his plans. Many have an idea that five acres of land will be enough; others put it at ten; while it is known that some cultivate a hundred acres or more at a profit. The amount of capital required varies, to some extent, with the amount of land cultivated but not in a uniform proportion; while a larger variation still will result from the greater or less provision we may choose to make in the matter of hot-houses. Not including these in the scheme of cultivation, and on the presumption that we are to do such forcing only as can be done in hot-beds, we may fix approximate amounts as follows, viz.:

While it might require about $3,000, with the labor of three men and two horses, to properly handle two acres, we estimate that there would be needed about $5,000, six men, and three horses for ten acres; and that $20,000, forty men, and twenty horses would be sufficient for one hundred acres.

One of the largest and most indispensable items of original outlay is in providing the sashes; these cost, with the requisite mats and shutters to go with them, about $4.00 each, of which about $2.50 is paid for the sash, and the balance for mats and shutters to correspond. But in a scheme combining, not only hot-bed and out-door cultivation, but forcing-houses as well, the possible outlay is, of course, almost unlimited.

A very important item of annual outlay is the supply of stable manure. This will cost, at present prices, delivered on the place, from $4.00 to $7.00 per cord, according to distance from the city and the facilities for obtaining and transporting it.

The land cultivated may be the gardener's own, or may be worked under a lease. In the latter case, the annual rent per acre is, at an average, say $25.00 for highly cultivated land, while other land in the remoter suburbs, and not in as good condition, might be had for $10.00 per year : — exclusive of buildings.

There may doubtless be found some tracts of land under cultivation where ordinary interest reckoned on the purchase money invested would amount to $200.00

or more annually, per acre; but these are, of course, exceptional cases.

With regard to the expense of labor, it may be stated that average men receive about $40.00 per month, or about $1.50 per day, during the summer season, and about $35.00 per month, or $1.35 per day, during the four months of winter. Of course skilled laborers might expect to receive more, but to obtain it they must be men of some experience and natural adaptation to the work. The business is one in which men of tact and experience are in demand, no less than in a manufacturing or mercantile establishment.

The expense of keeping the work-horses, including all items, would amount to about $150.00 on each animal per year. The tools are a less important item of expense, and yet the new and improved implements of the present date are quite costly, and the cultivation of even a limited amount of land requires quite a number of them.

By looking over the foregoing it will be seen that, if we exclude the more elaborate culture in hot-houses, the total annual expense of running two acres of land would be about $2,500. That of five acres would foot up about $5,000; of ten acres, about $8,000; while a hundred acres could be run for $25,000. Many people have a mistaken idea that they can run a garden of ten, fifteen, or twenty acres on a capital smaller than is really requisite to properly run three acres. If one's capital is limited, it is far better to proportionally reduce the amount of land and improve the culture by use of the best methods and appliances.

SUCCESS IN MARKET GARDENING.

Part II.

DIRECTIONS AND DESCRIPTIONS IN DETAIL.

Artichoke — Green Globe.

CHAPTER IV.

VEGETABLES RAISED FOR MARKET — CHARACTERISTICS — CULTURAL DIRECTIONS.

THE ARTICHOKE (*Cynara Scolymus*) is used extensively in Europe, either raw as a salad or boiled and served after the manner of cabbage. It may also be blanched somewhat as we treat endive — that is, the side stalks — and it is then used as a salad.

It may be propagated either from the seed or by root cuttings. The latter is the best and most convenient plan; the offset suckers should be taken in the spring. When raised from seed, let them be sown early in the spring, say at the time of the flowering of the peach, in drills a foot apart, and four inches apart in the drills. The next spring transplant to permanent beds, in hills three feet apart each way, with three plants to a hill. It requires a deep, rich loam, abounding in moisture.

As the plant is perennial, one planting will answer for several years. No winter protection will be required except in the most northern States, and there a coat of straw or leaves will suffice to insure them against winter killing.

The Green Globe and Common Green, which are

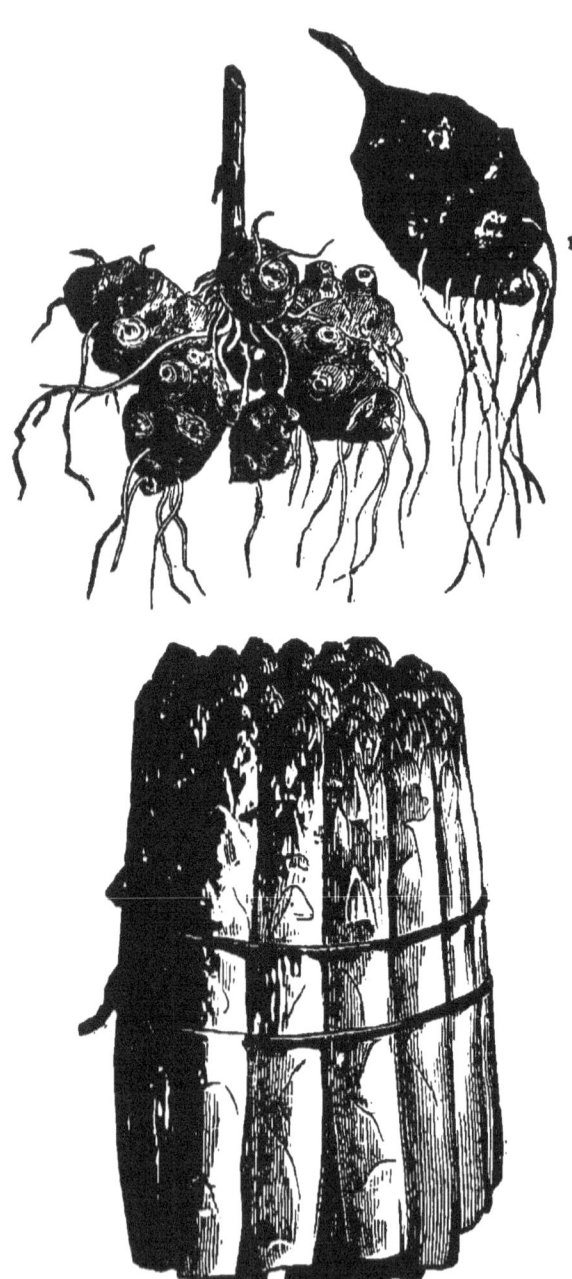

(1) Jerusalem Artichoke.   (2) Bunch of Asparagus.

much alike, are the varieties we have had in mind in writing the above, but there is another variety, called the Jerusalem Artichoke (*Helianthus tuberosus*), which differs from these in the fact that it is cultivated for its tubers, which are pickled like cucumbers or eaten raw sliced as a salad. They are planted like potatoes, in hills or rows, and will produce enormous crops. The tubers make excellent feed for all kinds of live stock, being the richest in fat-producing elements of any of our cultivated roots. Care must be taken at the time of harvesting to remove all the small roots, for if left in the ground they will come up the next spring, and may become a troublesome weed.

ASPARAGUS (*A. officinalis*) is a peculiar crop, and generally speaking is a reliable one. The fact that it takes two years from the setting if two-year-old plants are set, or four years if the seed is sown, prevents many from growing it. It is not generally grown in the immediate vicinity of Boston or other large cities, as the land is usually too valuable. The average proceeds per acre are moderate; from $200 to $300.

As compared with other crops, it is a good one to ship, and will stand up well for quite a length of time.

Asparagus is a hardy, perennial, maritime plant. It may be grown from seed, or propagated by roots. One ounce of seed will sow about fifty feet of drill. It will thrive on almost any sandy soil, even if quite light, and the lighter the soil, other things being equal, the earlier the crop may be got off. A planting once properly made will last for years. A fair crop may be expected the third year from the seed, or in one or two years from the roots, according to their age when planted, and, after that, full crops every year.

The soil for this crop cannot be made too rich, and should be thoroughly trenched two feet or more in depth. The plants should be set six to eight inches deep, in rows three to four feet apart, and one foot apart in the rows. The roots should be set in the spring as soon as the ground is in good working order (they can be set in the fall, but the spring is the preferable time), say about the end of April. The crowns of the roots should be from four to six inches from the surface of the bed. A heavy application of manure must be made to an asparagus bed each fall — say eight or ten cords per acre. This should be lightly worked into the soil in the spring: a very light surface-ploughing will accomplish this well, if carefully done. Salt is an excellent thing to apply for a dressing, for, although it does not act as a manure, as some people think, it is a great help in keeping down the weeds.

In cutting for market, the cut is made about two inches under the ground, and pains are taken to have the stalks about eight inches long. In preparing for market a buncher is used, so that all bunches are of exactly equal length and size. From twelve to twenty stalks are put in each bunch, according to the size of the stalks. They bring, on an average, about $1.50 per dozen bunches, still the price varies greatly with different seasons and depends largely on the supply of peas and greens that may be in the market. The season for cutting usually continues about five weeks, and the plants are then left to go to seed. In the fall if stable manure is to be applied, these seed stalks may be mown down and the ground cleared off by burning over; but in case commercial fertilizers are to be employed, it will be of advantage to let the stalks stand, for protection, mowing them down in the spring.

The varieties are numerous, and differ considerably. Conover's Colossal is quite popular; and Moore's New Giant Cross-bred is now the variety most in use.

As already said, the profit to be made from asparagus will not warrant its open-air culture upon the high-priced lands that lie near the markets where it must be sold; but, fortunately, it keeps well, and will bear transporting over long distances.

It has been somewhat out of favor with market gardeners, but it is now beginning to be forced in hot-houses, thus commanding a fancy price. Where it is grown in this way, the roots are dug in the fall and put into a cool cellar till required to be placed in the forcing-house. The asparagus will be fit for cutting in three or four weeks. The roots thus taken up are of no use after being forced in this manner.

BEANS (*Phaseolus vulgaris.*) — Dwarf or Bush kinds. This familiar crop flourishes best in a rather light, gravelly soil; and it should never be planted in very heavy land. Beans are extremely sensitive to frost and cold. The bush beans are rather more hardy than the pole varieties, but nevertheless should not be planted until settled weather; say, in this section, about the first week in May. Nothing is gained by putting them in when the weather is cold, or the land damp and soggy, for they are a crop that never recovers

Golden-Pod Yellow-Eyed Wax Bean.

DWARF OR BUSH — CULTURE — VARIETIES. 85

from a set-back received early in the season. Whenever the land has become light and warm, select a dry and sheltered location ; and on ground lightly manured, and in good condition of tilth, plant in drills or rows. Hoe often, but only when dry. Plant at intervals till the last of July for a succession.

In manuring for this crop, we have found it works well to give the land a fair dressing of manure (lightly worked into the soil) and then give a light application of some fertilizer, say wood ashes, or Bowker's Special Phosphate, in the drill at the time of planting. This seems to give the crop a quicker and better start than it gets where manure is applied directly in the drill. The distance apart for the rows should be from three to three and a half feet, and the seed dropped from four to six inches apart in the drill (which should be from an inch to an inch and a half in depth). At this distance apart, about one bushel of seed would be required per acre, where all the land is devoted to the crop ; but many prefer to plant every fourth row with squash, so as to double-crop the land.

A fair average yield per acre would be from three hundred to four hundred bushels ; and the crop ought to bring from seventy cents to one dollar per bushel. A good picker should pick two and a half barrels per day, or about eight bushels.

After the crop is fairly up, the cultivator should be run through lightly ; and, at the second hoeing, a little earth should be drawn toward the plants to support them. They should never be hoed or worked amongst, if it can possibly be avoided, at times when they are wet, either by rain or dew, as there is much danger of rusting or blighting the crop.

The list of varieties is numerous and contains many of real merit. The Early Long Yellow Six Weeks is the earliest good market variety, of first-rate quality and excellent in every respect. Its pods are green. The Early Mohawk is another good kind, closely resembling the Six Weeks in habit. It is nearly or quite as early, and is also a green-podder. Dwarf Yellow Cranberry is another excellent green-podded variety, a trifle later than the above, but of excellent quality, and a favorite snap bean for the market.

Golden-pod Yellow-eyed Wax. This superb variety is a leading sort, both for the market and home garden. It is certainly the very best wax bean in cultivation, and has never been known to spot, which is a common defect of wax beans. Golden Wax is good, but has the fault of spotting. In both varieties the pods are of a rich golden-yellow; they are stringless and of fine flavor; both varieties are exceedingly productive, and are not surpassed in this respect by any. Black Wax resembles the Golden, but is a trifle later; its pods are round instead of flattened.

The White Wax is waxen-podded, very tender, and of good quality. This is a favorite with many for the home garden. The Early Valentine is undoubtedly an excellent variety, of a tender and succulent growth. It is not very much cultivated in this vicinity, but only because it happens to be less generally known here than in other parts of the country.

The Dwarf Horticultural is the standard market

variety, and is the leading dwarf Shell Bean. Pod very plump and large, streaked with bright red. The Goddard is a splendid variety, somewhat later than the above, but of excellent quality, and very prolific. The pods are of a brighter red than the Horticultural, and the yield is heavier.

Ruby Horticultural is just introduced; is similar to the last-named, but has a redder and brighter pod, somewhat flatter in shape.

The *Pole* or *Running* kinds are less hardy than the bush varieties, and will not bear planting quite as early. From about the middle of May to the first of June, according to the season, is about right with us.

They should invariably be planted in hills, which should be about three feet apart, with rows four feet apart. From five to six seeds should be placed in each hill, with the eye downward, and should be covered to about the same depth as is directed for bush or snap beans. A quart of seed will plant a hundred and fifty hills; the poles should be set at the time of planting.

They succeed best in sandy loam, which should be liberally enriched with short manure in the hills. Three plants in a hill are as many as should be allowed to grow, and, with the vigorous growing kinds on strong soil, it is better to have only two. The thinning should be done when the plants have become well established. They bear transplanting well, and this affords a means of filling up around the poles where they miss or fail to come up. They can also be started in frames and transplanted to the open ground, so as to secure an advanced stage of growth and earlier maturity; but this method is not extensively practised. The maturity of some of the later sorts can be hastened by nipping off the tips of the runners when they have reached the height of four or five feet.

The Brockton pole bean is one of late introduction; has long, dark-red pods; is highly productive, and, in this vicinity, the most popular kind at present.

Red Cranberry is an excellent variety, of good quality, productive, and stringless. The pods retain their tender and palatable quality until they are quite enough grown to shell beans. As a shell bean it is good while green; but is not often used after ripening and drying.

White Cranberry is very similar to the above variety, but not quite as productive. Some prefer it, however, on account of its being a white bean.

Pole Horticultural has perhaps a greater combination of good qualities than any other pole variety. It is excellent as a string bean, unsurpassed for shelling green, and, moreover, is one of the best varieties on the list for cooking in the dry state.

Indian Chief. — This bean is remarkable for its tender, succulent, and richly colored pods, and is well worthy a place in every garden. It is a very productive sort. The pods remain tender and crisp a long time. The seeds are not often used in the dry state — in fact, as a rule, no black beans are used dry — but for a string Pole Bean this variety has no superior.

Scarlet Runner (*P. multiflorus*) is rather late, and should be planted as early as possible. In this country it is produced mostly as an ornamental climbing plant.

Lima Beans (*P. lunatus*) are very tender, and should

be planted after the ground is warm and mellow, say about the first of June. Or they may be started earlier in hot-beds, like cucumbers and melons, and transplanted to the open ground at about the time stated.

Dreer's Improved Lima is a little earlier than the old Lima; very productive. The beans form very closely in the pod, and are of excellent quality and flavor. Sieva, or Small Lima, is smaller than the above, but cannot be excelled in quality.

THE BEET (*Beta vulgaris*) is one of the most important crops, and is of easy culture. Where possible, a rather light, sandy loam should be selected for this crop, in preference to heavy soil. For the early crop, the seed should be put in about the middle of April, or as soon as the ground is in a suitable working condition. The rows should be planted by machine, at distances of from twelve to fourteen inches apart, and the drills should be one inch deep. After they have gained a foothold the plants should be thinned to eight or ten inches apart in the drill. Clean culture should of course be given, and the soil well enriched.

The above remarks apply to the crop when grown for early marketing. For winter use the seed should be sown about the first of July, in drills drawn at the same distances apart as above directed, but the plants should be left nearer together, say at intervals of from five to six inches.

Of varieties there are a large number known and named, but few of really superior merit. We recommend the Early Crosby Egyptian for earliest, and for forcing; then the Bastian, with the Arlington Favorite

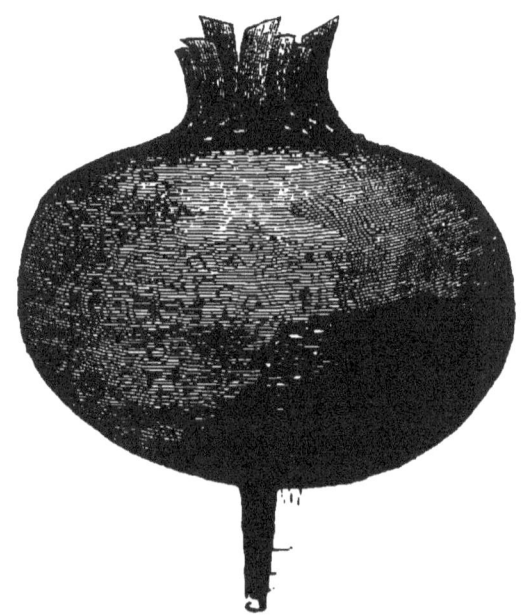
Crosby's Improved Egyptian.

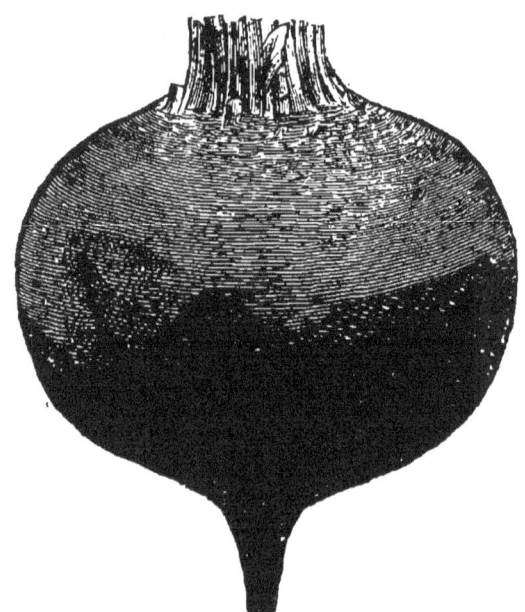
Arlington Favorite

(next in earliness to the Bastian) and Dewing Blood Turnip, and Edmands — all these three being true blood beets — for standard sorts. The early Bastian is one of the very earliest, and is one of the best as regards quality. It is not a true blood beet, but is sweet and of very good quality the year round.

The three that we have selected as standard sorts are well marked and very distinct in type. Rawson's Arlington Favorite is really the most thoroughly fixed in type; has deep blood-red flesh of excellent flavor, exceedingly sweet and tender; is shapely in form, with very smooth skin, and of good market size. It is a new and very superior variety, one that serves equally well for bunching and for the general crop.

The Dewing is also of fine form and flavor, of a fairly good color, and free from fibrous roots.

The Edmands is another market-gardener's strain, of great regularity in shape, deep blood skin, and very dark flesh of superior quality.

Dark Red Egyptian is a very early variety, but there are a great many that believe the Bastian, and also the Eclipse, to be equally early. In shape it is much flattened, color deep crimson, top small. It is certainly very early, and very good when small; but when full grown is woody and of poor quality.

Eclipse is a blood beet, very fine grained, of good shape, and good at all seasons of the year. It is extremely popular among market gardeners; has dark-red flesh and skin; is almost spherical in form.

The *Swiss Chard* is a peculiar sort. It is cultivated mainly for the stem and midrib of the leaf, which may

92   MARKET GARDENING.

Swiss Chard.

Dwarf Siberian Kale.

be boiled and served like asparagus, and the strippings can be used as spinach. When gathered it should be cut close down to the ground, and new growth will sprout up. It is hardly ever seen in this market.

The early beets are nearly always bunched, instead of being sold by the bushel. They are pulled when grown to about the circumference of a silver dollar, and are tied four in a bunch. The bunches usually bring from four to five cents each, and are sold by the dozen or hundred. At this price a good crop of early beets would bring returns of from $400 to $500 per acre. The thinnings are saved and sold for greens, by the bushel, like spinach. Late beets are, of course, sold by the bushel. A fair average yield, per acre, would be about 300 bushels, which ought to bring at least $150.

In southern New England such early varieties as the Early Bastian, Eclipse, or Egyptian, can be sown the second time on the same ground each season, and two crops per year can be raised; but with the later varieties, which require about two weeks longer to mature, the season would not be long enough.

Beets of the early varieties also make a first-rate second crop to follow peas, early cabbage, or any other early crop that is off the ground so that the beets can be put in by the 20th of July.

The amount of seed required, per acre, for the early crop (to be thinned for greens) is eight pounds. For the late crop, six pounds is the proper quantity.

BORECOLE, or KALE (*Brassica oleracea acephala*) is a name applied to the class of cabbage which does not head, but is used as an esculent in its open growth. When used, the crown or centre of the plant is cut off so as to include the leaves, which usually do not exceed nine inches in length. It boils well, and is more tender, sweet, and delicate, provided it has been duly exposed to frost. To secure heavy crops of this hardy, useful winter vegetable, a deep, rich soil is essential, and the ground should be trenched two feet deep and liberally manured. Sow about the middle of April, in well prepared soil, covering the seeds thinly and evenly. Half an ounce will sow a bed of twenty square feet. Plant out in June, and cultivate as elsewhere recommended for cabbage.

Dwarf Purple or Brown Kale.

The Dwarf Purple, or Brown Kale, which is represented in the cut here inserted, is a beautiful curled variety, with reddish-tinted leaves. Another is the Green Curled Scotch, which is very hardy, and, like the Savoys, is improved by a moderate frost.

In cultivating the Improved Siberian variety — a strain of the kind known as German Greens, or "sprouts" — sow in September, in rows one foot apart, and treat the same as spinach. This is a very hardy kind, much grown by the New York gardeners.

BROCCOLI (*Brassica oleracea Botrytis*) is a variety of cabbage very closely resembling the cauliflower. There is scarcely any difference between the two beyond what would naturally be looked for between different varieties. It is hardy, and sure to head, but is inferior in flavor.

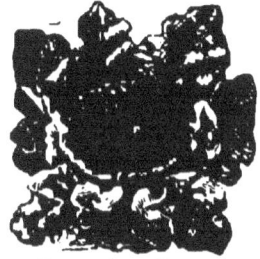
Purple Cap Broccoli.

All the varieties of Broccoli require a rich, deep soil; and the ground should be trenched to a depth of at least two feet, well incorporating, as the work proceeds, abundance of rich manure. Where the object is to obtain fine large heads, too much manure can hardly be used.

The seed should be sown in hot-beds, for early crops, in March or April; for main crops, in the open ground in May, in beds of well-pulverized rich soil, making the surface fine, and then beating the seed gently into the ground, and covering it with fine earth.

One ounce will sow a bed of forty square feet, and produce about 3,000 plants. When the plants are sufficiently strong, and before they are drawn by growing too closely together, transplant them into nursery beds or lines, allowing about four inches between the plants. This will insure strong, stocky plants, and will also induce the formation of an extra quantity of roots.

Plant in permanent situations as soon as the plants are sufficiently established, taking care not to injure the roots, in rows from two feet to two feet six inches apart, leaving about the same distance between the plants. Keep them well supplied with water until they get fairly established, especially the early varieties, and these must also be liberally watered in all stages of their growth during dry hot weather.

Keep the ground well stirred between the rows, and free from weeds. When they begin to flower, break the large leaves over the heads to protect them from the sun, and gather them before they commence running up to seed. Broccoli thrives best in cool, moist, fall weather,— hot, dry summer weather not being suited to it. The heads are cooked the same as cauliflower.

English seedsmen catalogue an almost endless number of varieties, but there are only a very few of distinct and admitted merit. Walcheren is an excellent variety, with large white heads. Early Purple Cap is an excellent sort; but many do not like the greenish-purple color of the heads. White Cap is, perhaps, our best variety; heads very white and solid,— a sure header.

This vegetable is not raised extensively in any section of this country, except in California.

BRUSSELS SPROUTS (*Brassica oleracea bullata*).—This is yet another of the Cabbage family, and like Broccoli is little grown here, though its excellent qualities seem to be fully appreciated by our English cousins. The culture is simple, and very much the same as

BRUSSELS SPROUTS.

is adopted for cauliflower or cabbage (except that it must be remembered that the Sprouts are a little less hardy). A similar quantity of seed is required.

The seeds should be sown in March or April in the hot-bed, or in the open ground when the weather permits. When the plants are about three inches high they should be transplanted. The early ones will be ready for the table in September; the late ones, for winter use, should be harvested before cold weather, and stored the same as cabbages or cauliflowers.

Brussels Sprouts

The small heads, which grow along the stem, are the eatable parts of this vegetable, and when boiled like cabbage, or stewed with cream, like cauliflower, are very tender and delicious. Where the winters are not very severe, they may remain in the ground, to be cut as needed; in fact, the sprouts are much improved by a moderate frost. The leaves, which resemble the Savoy, should be broken down in the fall to give the little cabbages room to grow.

Rawson's Volunteer.

Rawson's Early Summer.

Dwarf Improved is very tender and is distinguished for fine flavor; it is the best kind for general use.

CABBAGE (*Brassica oleracea capitata*) is one of the most important and one of the best paying crops.

Lettuce can be set between the cabbage rows, to be cut off before the growth of the main crop will interfere with it. In this manner three crops may be grown each season; which will make the land pay as well as can be done by almost any other system of cropping.

As cabbages require a large amount of lime, they should not be grown on the same ground oftener than once in three years, unless a special application of lime is made. This is often done, and especially in the vicinity of New York City; but, where practicable, it is better to avoid devoting the ground continuously to crops of the cabbage family. And it is also better to avoid putting in cabbages to follow any shallow-feeding crop (like corn, for instance) as they collect the greater part of their nourishment near the surface, and are moreover rank feeders; so that it is well to let them follow and be followed by some deep-rooted crop.

On land already in good tillable condition, an application of twenty cords of manure per acre is about what will be required. We prefer well decomposed horse manure to any other. This manure may cost about $7.00 per cord, delivered on the place.

The applying would cost about $6.00; ploughing, $2.00; marking, or furrowing, $2.00; setting, or transplanting, $5.00; hoeing, $5.00 (which would include cultivating); plants (6,000 at $5.00 per thousand),

$30.00; rent, $25.00; marketing, $25.00; making a total of $240.00.

If set at intervals of three and a half feet by two feet, the number of plants that can be grown per acre is six thousand. And it thus appears that they cannot be grown at smaller actual cost than four cents per head. The general average price is only six cents, which would indicate a profit of only $120 per acre; although, of course, if they should bring eight or ten cents, as they often do, the profit would be handsomely increased.

It will be seen that we have charged all the twenty cords of manure to the cabbages, while in fact the cabbages only take a share of it, and usually leave an abundance for the crop that follows. So it becomes a rather difficult matter to figure the exact cost by itself of growing a field of cabbages; but after the second crop is harvested it will be an easy affair to distribute the expenses between the two, and thus one may get at the matter very closely.

If it is seen that the manure which has been applied is not sufficient to carry out the crop, a dressing should be given of half a ton of some good commercial fertilizer that is rich in potash. Wood-ashes, when obtainable, are excellent for this purpose.

Rawson's Volunteer is the newest variety offered and is the earliest. In a test made on our trial grounds at Arlington, it was ready for marketing fully eight or ten days in advance of any other. It bears a striking resemblance to the French variety known as the Etampes, also an extremely early sort; the heads are firm and solid, and the leaves grow in very compact form, so that they may be planted very close.

Although the list of varieties is large, market gardeners have but few that they regard as reliable. The Jersey Wakefield is really the early market cabbage, and is undoubtedly cultivated to a greater extent than any other one variety for the first early crop. Although this sort is a few days later than the very earliest, it is enough larger to make up for the difference in time, and is usually more profitable than the smaller kinds.

Rawson's Early Summer excels both in size and earliness, and ranks as the best of the early Drumhead sorts. It is a trifle larger than the Wakefield, and consequently the setting should be a little farther apart. We would not advise setting any closer than three and a half feet for the rows, and plants at twenty inches, as this will give them none too much room. And although they may be, and in some cases are, planted closer, it is not so desirable, especially in this market.

The wider planting is better, even in places where cabbages are sold entirely by weight. We do not doubt that by setting at two feet apart each way just as many pounds per acre could be raised ; but the advantage in the wider style of planting is that less plants will be required per acre, and consequently there will be less work in cutting ; and further the cabbages will usually be harder and of better quality.

The Early Etampes is earlier by about ten days than any other cabbage excepting the newly catalogued

Volunteer. The heads are oblong, rounded at the top, and of medium size; they are very solid and firm and of good quality.

Fottler's Early Brunswick is a very popular variety some two weeks later than the Early Summer.

The Short-Stem Drumhead conforms very well to its name, having a remarkably short stem. The heads are very large, hard and solid, round, flattened on top and grow very uniform in size and shape. They fre-

Short-Stem Drumhead.

quently attain a weight of twenty or thirty pounds, and are always of the finest quality. It is a sure header.

The Curled Savoy ranks along the latest: and is grown mostly for winter use. The Globe Curled is the popular Curled Savoy cabbage of the Boston market. The Drumhead Savoy, which is a cross of the Globe Curled and Drumhead, is a large-headed Savoy cabbage, tender and fine-flavored, a good winter variety. It differs from the Curled in being of larger size and less curled. As a Savoy it is less desirable than the smaller variety for eating, but the crop is a profitable one to raise. It is a good variety for winter use.

The Savoy cabbages have wrinkled leaves and have a peculiar flavor that is much liked by most people. They are improved in quality by a slight touch of frost. The Globe curled variety, before named, is an

Globe Curled Savoy.

American sort. English Curled Savoy is a peculiar sort used for early spring greens.

For the early varieties, which we have mentioned above, the seed is usually sown in hot-beds, from the 10th to the 20th of February. They should be covered about half an inch deep. In about four weeks they are ready for transplanting, which is usually done in a bed from which a crop of lettuce has just been removed. They should be put in about three and a half inches apart, so as to give them plenty of room to grow stout and stocky. By this rule two hundred plants are put under each sash. After they have obtained a good start the sash should be removed gradually, to allow them to harden off; and they may be given all the protection necessary in severe weather by the use of shutters. They are usually transplanted to the open ground either the last week in April or the first in May, according to the season.

The land best suited to this crop is a deep rich loamy soil, and should be prepared by very heavy manuring; lap two furrows together about three and one half feet apart and beat them down nearly level with a fork. A sprinkling of wood ashes on the young plants will keep off the cabbage-fly, and promote their growth.

For late crops, sow from June 1 to June 20, and even as late as the 1st of July, in the field, or in beds, so as to transplant. Cover three quarters of an inch deep, as the soil is drier now than earlier in the season. Shade and water the late sowings in dry weather to get them up.

It is important that the plants should stand thinly in the seed bed, or they will run up weak and slender, and be likely to make long stumps. When the weather is hot and dry the roots of the plants may be dipped in a puddle of loam and water, and transplanted just at evening, giving each plant a gill of water at the root. If planting seed in hills twenty-two inches apart, plant six or eight seeds; of such as come up, reserve one and transplant the rest.

Late cabbages are usually grown as a second crop, following peas or something similar in culture; or they may be set on newly turned land which has been in early grain or grass. It is not generally necessary to apply as much manure as for the early crop; twelve cords is usually an abundant dressing, especially where they follow some other crop which has been well manured the same season.

To keep cabbage through the winter, commence by making a small bank, say about one and a half feet high, in some sheltered locality. Pull the cabbage, and place the heads against the bank in a row as close as they can stand; then turn up the earth with the plow against the row. Be careful not to cover the head, but make the earth firm around the roots. Then with a shovel square down the bank thus made, and place another row; this will be about eight or ten inches from the first, and so continue until the whole are set out. Another way is to place the cabbages head downwards on the ground, and cover the heads and stumps with dirt, then adding hay or something similar to keep out the frost. This protection should also be given in banking up by the other method. Put on enough to be sure that they will not freeze solid. If frozen about half through, they are not injured, and will keep quite well. Some have houses where they store the cabbages, placing them head down on the shelf, laying them as close as possible, and only one deep. The temperature is kept at about the freezing point.

CARROT (*Daucus carota*) is perhaps more properly to be called a farm crop; still, to some extent, it is grown by market gardeners who chance to be located near large cities, and yet on land that is not too valuable. They require a very finely pulverized and porous sandy loam for their full development, and for large crops. It is important that the land should not be too rich, as then the crop will run too much to tops; and still they should not be placed on poor, light soil with the expectation of a big crop. Land that is in fairly good condition, and has been manured the year previous for some other crop, is usually quite rich enough for the growing of carrots.

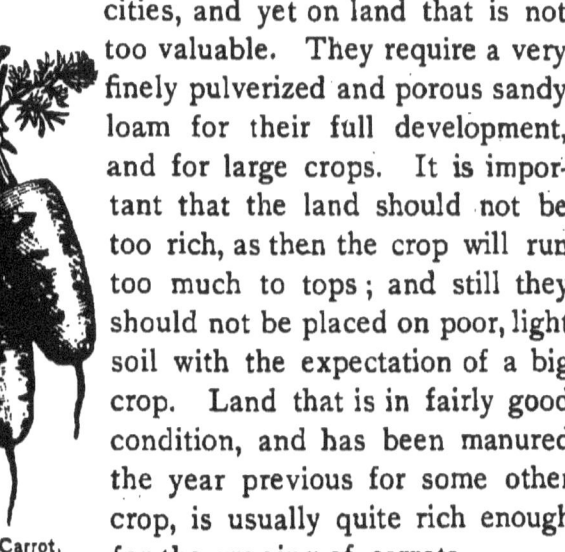

Early Horn Carrot.

When the short varieties (like Early Horn, Intermediate, etc.) are raised for bunching, they are usually put in as a second crop with spring spinach and radishes. They are tied in bunches, four in a bunch, like early beets; and usually bring, on an average, four cents per bunch. But there is only a limited demand for them.

When grown under glass, they are usually raised as a third crop in the following manner: After a crop of lettuce has been removed from the bed, perhaps

French Early Forcing.

about the first of February, the ground is sown to radishes and carrots, putting the latter in every third row — so that there are two rows of radishes to one of carrots. About the last week in March the radishes are ready for pulling, which leaves the carrots in full possession of the beds. The Early French Forcing is the leading variety for hot-bed culture. The plants have but a very small top, run very even in size, and are of good appearance.

Early Scarlet Horn.

The sash, being usually removed some time between March 20 and April, can after that date be used for some other purpose, and, until warm weather all the protection needed by the carrots may be given with shutters.

They will be ready for pulling and bunching about the last week in May (taking for their growth about twice the time of the radishes). At this season they will usually bring on an average $1.00 per dozen bunches, five carrots being put in a bunch, and at this price the crop will bring about $1.50 per sash.

For out-door culture the Early Scarlet Horn or Butter is the earliest variety, and can be sown either as a separate crop or with others. This is a stump root variety, and is grown exclusively for bunching.

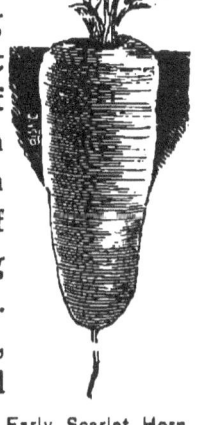

Danvers Half Long.

The Danvers Half Long Orange is the standard main crop variety; being usually sold by the barrel, box, or bushel, for fall and winter use. It is a remarkably prolific variety, yielding frequently (and in some instances considerably) over forty tons per acre. It is withal an excellent keeper.

The Thick Half Long Orange is an excellent strain of the ordinary Improved Long Orange, and is extensively grown in field culture; but is not as desirable, except for stock feeding, as the Danvers. The Improved Long Orange is the standard stock carrot. The roots are large and long, and are of good quality for feeding. The Large White Belgian is used for stock only. As the crown of this carrot grows five or six inches out of ground, they are more easily dug than any other sort; and are liked by many on this account. The Long Scarlet Antringham is a very irregular shaped red variety. It is less productive and is no better in any way than the Long Orange.

Improved Long Orange Carrot.

CAULIFLOWER (*Brassica oleracea Botrytis*). The culture of this crop involves much painstaking labor;

nevertheless, in the vicinity of Boston, the acreage devoted to cauliflower has been largely increased over that of ten years ago. Fields as large as eight or ten acres are not uncommon. When grown in large quantities they are usually stored in the fall for winter marketing. They are one of the various forms of the cabbage family and require similar general treatment.

In the ordinary Cabbage, which is a biennial plant, the rounded, thick, fleshy, strongly veined leaves afford the edible portion; being collected into a head the first year, at the summit of a short and stout stem. In Cauliflower, and similarly in Broccoli, the nutritive matter mainly concentrates in short, imperfect flower branches collected into a flattish head.

It is naturally a fall crop, and will not well bear early forcing, although the heads are now grown to some extent in hot-houses, out of season, thus commanding high prices. They are more or less subject to club-root; as to the cause and remedy for which there is not yet much satisfactory information; and there are other limitations to their profitable culture which gardeners have not yet perfectly learned. The culture of this vegetable has increased in this vicinity; but some think there has been a decline, in the country taken as a whole, in recent years.

In out-door culture, when they do well they will usually pay better than early cabbage; but there is much more risk in cultivating them. As raised in this locality, about six thousand are grown per acre, and if maturing well will bring in about $700.00. The price varies from $1.00 to $2.00 per dozen.

They are usually grown, like late cabbage, for a second crop. Sometimes a piece of land is devoted solely to them through the season; but when set early they do not usually head as well. From the first of May until the first of July, according to the date when plants will be wanted for setting, is the time to put in the seed. It is a crop that well repays generous treatment in cultivation. With a deep rich soil well supplied with moisture, which in dry seasons must be artificially furnished, cauliflowers can be grown well. Frequent hoeing and a liberal supply of rich liquid manure, to keep up a continuous and rapid growth, will produce splendid heads of the most delicate flavor. It facilitates blanching if the leaves are gathered loosely together, and tied over the top of the head to protect from the sun. They must be taken before the flowers begin to open.

There is no garden crop that is pinched more severely by a drought than the cauliflower; and none, perhaps, which will pay better for irrigation.

Sowing for plants of the very earliest varieties may be done in houses or hot-beds in February or March; or later in a cold frame. Sow as late as June 20 or July 1, for late crops, in beds or in hills, covering one half inch deep. For the early fall crop, sow in May and transplant in June, in rows four feet apart, setting the plants two feet apart in the row; water frequently if the ground be dry.

As directed for cabbage culture — give the young plants special attention, if the weather be hot and dry at the time of transplanting, and use means already described to prevent injury resulting from their roots becoming in the least dry from exposure to sun or air. Transplant at evening as far as practicable; and always choose a moist day rather than a dry one, if circumstances permit a choice.

The young plants are frequently attacked by a little black beetle, but its ravages may be stopped by frequent applications of plaster dusted on in the morning while the dew is on.

For the main crop, early variety, there is with us nothing so good as Rawson's Sea Foam, which derives its name from the pure white color of the heads. It is quite distinct and the surest header we know of. The Snowball, being a very sure header, is quite desirable, although not equalling the Sea Foam with us. The Early Dwarf Erfurt is one of the standard varieties, and used both for early and late sowings. It is a very sure header, not large, but even in size. The Late Erfurt is a later strain of the preceding, and consequently requires a longer season to reach maturity. It is large in size. The Algiers is a splendid sort, the largest and latest of all the varieties grown. It is the kind most in use for pickling, because of its superior size and weight.

CELERIAC or Turnip-Rooted Celery (*Apium graveolens rapaceum*), although but little used in this country, is quite popular in Europe, especially in Germany and France. It is rather peculiar in its manner of growth. It is started, and in its early stages should be treated, precisely like celery, except that, as it requires but a slight earthing up, the plants may be set much closer.

Two feet apart for the rows, and eight inches for the plants, will give abundance of room. The sowing should be done early in the spring in light, rich soil; transplant in May into beds and water freely in dry weather. The earthing up is done when the plants are nearly full grown and the bulbs should be covered

Celeriac.

to a depth of four or five inches. In about a month they will have become sufficiently blanched. The globe-shaped bulbous roots form the edible portion, and are commonly ready for use in October. For winter use they may be stored in trenches after the manner in which celery is kept; or placed in sand in a cool cellar.

They are used on the table in various ways; they may be put into soups; or sliced and used with vinegar, making a most excellent salad; or cooked by boiling, after being scraped and sliced, till they have become very tender, after which they are stewed in just milk enough to cover, then seasoned with salt and served with butter. A very productive variety is known as "Apple-Shaped;" very regular, almost spherical in form, with a fine neck and small leaves; it may be planted very thickly and will yield a heavy crop. It is botanically classed as a kind of celery, and is often catalogued by seedsmen as a variety of that plant.

CELERY (*Apium graveolens*).— Although the culture of this crop has become widely extended, and the amount of annual product has vastly increased of late years and is still continually increasing, it is none the less a fact that the profitable management of it is a matter of exceeding difficulty. The crop is one that demands more careful and laborious attention than almost any other in the market-gardener's list.

The seed is extremely small and remarkably slow in germinating, and this presents at the outset one of the difficulties of celery-growing, viz., securing a good stand of plants to commence with. To accomplish this demands, amongst other things, a seed-bed well and thoroughly prepared, a careful choice of the most suitable varieties and a skilful sowing of well-selected seed.

In choosing a place for starting the plants, find

if possible a cool and partially shaded spot. The soil should be put in good condition and firmed down. After it is prepared in this respect, rake the surface lightly and sow on the seed broadcast, then place a hot-bed shutter, or a plank, on the surface, and have a man walk or jump upon it until the soil is again well compacted. After this, sift on soil, using just enough to cover the seed lightly, not over a quarter of an inch at most. Then pat down moderately with the back of a spade or shovel, and the work is done, except watering, until the plants are well up, which will usually be at the end of three or four weeks' time. The bed should be kept constantly moist, but not too wet. An ounce of seed should sow a space about six feet square, and should furnish fully six thousand plants. The seed does not suffer from age until it is over five years old.

In describing the foregoing method we have assumed that the plants are to be lifted and transplanted, but many growers sow the seed in the rows where the crop is to stand. On many accounts we prefer the former plan. You will always get a much more even and generally a more vigorous stand, by transplanting, than when the plants have grown from seed sown in the field and have been cultivated by thinning out; and the former plan has been found in our experience to succeed the best all the way through. Still, since the results of the same experiments will often vary in different localities and under differing conditions, it may be well for any one to try both methods, and to follow up the trial far enough to perceive which it is that seems the one best adapted to his own situation. Much may be found to depend upon the natural quality of the soil — its condition of tilth and general preparation — the risks resulting from the vicissitudes of the weather, etc. Yet the fact remains that it is usually much better and easier to transplant a crop trom the seed-bed than to thin out a standing one, and the plants so established will exhibit a more uniform growth.

When the celery is to follow cabbage or other early crops, the plants are usually twice transplanted ; — once from the seed-bed, and again when set out permanently in the open field. When lifted from the seed-bed, they are put out five or six inches apart, so that, when next to be removed they can be lifted singly, and without their being so violently disturbed as when lifted from a bed where they have grown to large size standing close, and with roots all twined together.

In this section, celery is invariably grown as a second or third crop. The soil best adapted to celery is a strong deep sandy loam, naturally moist; the crop needs and must have plenty of moisture during droughts, or a shortage will be the inevitable result.

When celery is to follow early cabbage, it is the usual custom to plough the land before setting the plants. But no manure should be applied beyond that already in the soil. Experience proves that the land is usually able to carry out the crop better by relying upon the unconsumed portion of the fertilizers supplied to the earlier crop than by addition of fresh manure.

Care must be taken to set the plants at just the

right depth — just so deep as not to cover the crown — and the loosened soil must be pressed down and brought together firmly about the roots. Celery of all kinds should be planted for level culture, and not in trenches.

We have usually had the rows six feet apart, and plants one foot apart in the row. The only cultivation necessary after the setting, until it is time for the hilling-up, — usually termed banking, — consists in keeping the ground free from weeds and the surface mellow. Never hoe or bank when wet.

Where the celery is set out for a late crop, and is to be banked but once, the plants may in that case be set in rows only four and a half feet apart. The first transplanting is to be done in June, the second in July; sometimes, in a very wet season, it may be successful if as late as the first week in August.

If the crop has been planted out early, banking may begin the first week in September, or about four weeks before it is wanted. Two bankings will suffice for the early crop, and they should be timed about ten days apart. For later use, say about Thanksgiving time, commence about the first of October; repeat the banking about the tenth, and still again about the twentieth. For winter use, bank about the fifteenth or later, according to the season; and if the celery is not very large, one banking will be sufficient, as it only requires to be straightened up to have it keep long; and it is better if blanched but very little.

When it is ready for storing it should be taken up and placed in pits prepared for the purpose. The roots should be covered the same as if they were standing in the ground; and should be placed about six inches apart, if they are to remain on hand long, so as to allow the air to circulate properly.

To prepare a pit for storing celery make the sides of plank, 24 feet apart and about two feet high from the ground. The boards for covering should be thirteen feet long, the ends of two lengths meeting each other on the centre of the pit; where it should have an interior height of six feet. Enough loam is thrown out from the inside, in forming the pit, to embank the sides and ends.

In setting the celery, commence at one end of the pit: dig a trench about three inches deep, and set in the celery as closely as you can in the row. In taking up loam for covering the roots of one row, another trench is obtained for setting down the next. Be careful to make it stand up perfectly straight: and, either in the field or in the pit, the yellow leaves should all be removed before the packing in.

The pit can be extended to any length desired, and partitions may be employed: so that portions of the stock can be kept cooler, and so held back; or can be kept warmer and ripened off.

The pit coverings of boards must be put on as fast as the celery is got in. Small ventilators, about one foot square, are constructed along the centre, about twenty feet apart. These are opened in clear and moderately cold weather; and thus the temperature is kept at about 35° to 40° Fahrenheit, until a supply is wanted for market—when they can be kept closed, and the celery allowed to ripen.

The best material with which to cover the celery for long keeping is salt hay; but it can be ripened quickest under seaweed, which packs very closely when wet. One foot in thickness is sufficient for its protection if the outside thermometer does not go below zero. Some old mats or shutters may be put on for a short time when the weather is very cold. Thermometers should be provided, — one to be kept near each end; and, if the pit is one hundred feet long, or more, one will be needed in the middle.

In taking up loam for covering the roots of one row, another trench is obtained for setting down the next. A space of about six inches is usually left between each row and the next, to afford an air circulation; but, if the lot is not required to remain on hand long, this space is not necessary, and the rows may be brought close together. As much dirt as possible may be left on the roots, and it will keep all the better. The roots only should be covered with the loam, and no part of the stalk. It should not be put into the pit in a wet condition if it is intended to have it remain there for any long time.

The list of varieties is large; but still, as in the case of many other vegetables, there are but few of really superior merit. Rawson's Early Arlington has been decidedly the leading variety in the Boston market. It is first class in quality, and fully three weeks earlier than the old stand-by known as the Boston Market variety; grows larger, and yields more profit.

Sandringham Dwarf White is an excellent dwarf variety, of an upright habit of growth. Carter's

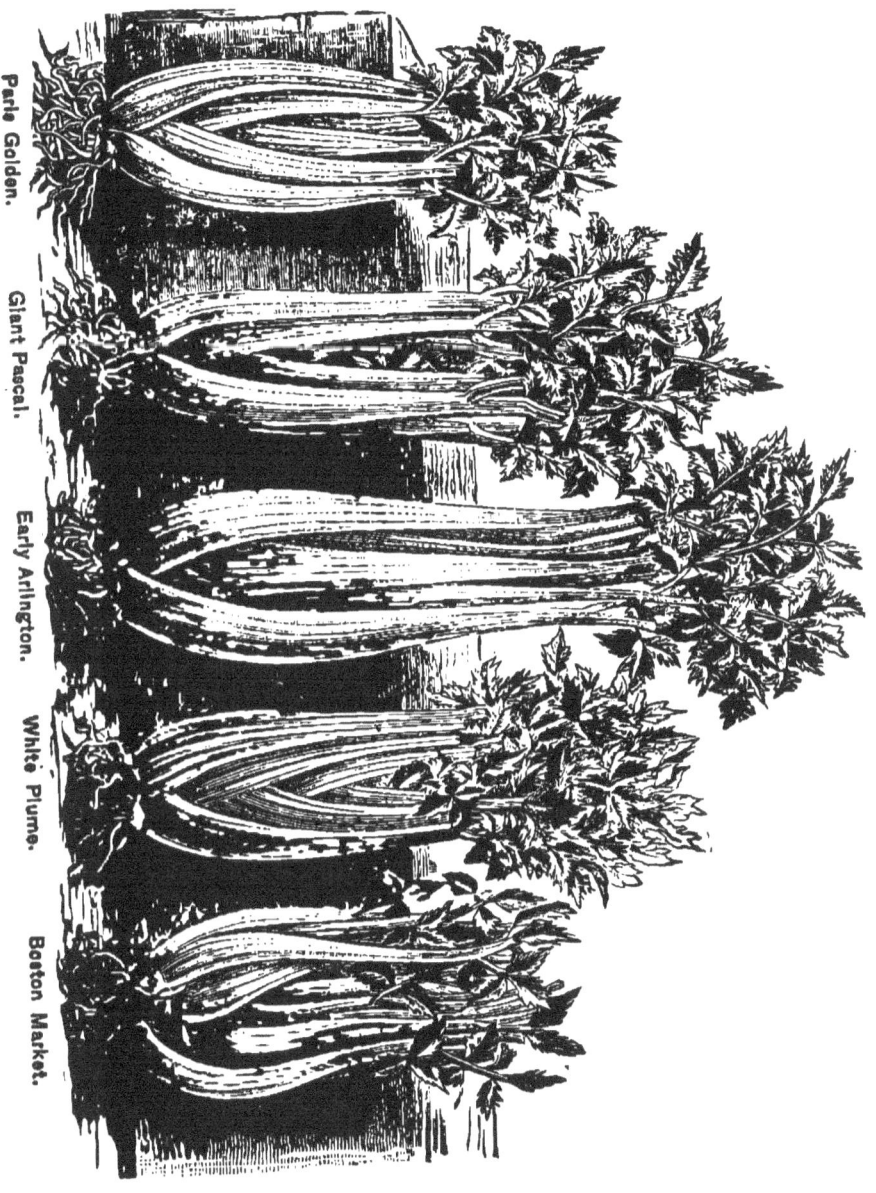

Crimson is a very dwarf, solid variety, crisp and tender — first class as a red variety. Henderson's Half Dwarf is somewhat similar to Crawford's; when blanched, it is of a yellow tinge, crisp, and of an agreeable, though rather peculiar nutty flavor. The White Plume is a noted dwarf variety, with a very marked peculiarity in the foliage. It is very white, and, being rather tender, is not an extra keeper. It bleaches easily, and needs rather less earthing up than some other kinds.

The Golden Heart celery is grown mostly by gardeners in the celery region of Kalamazoo, and is set in rows four and one-half feet apart, and four inches apart in the row; but it takes from six to twelve of their roots to make one of ours. They get about one cent per root for their celery, and we sell ours for prices ranging from five to twenty-five cents per root.

The varieties now most in favor are Paris Golden, White Plume, Giant Pascal, Arlington, and Boston Market. The first named is grown for earliest. The plants may stand quite close in the row — at six or eight inches apart, and with rows only three feet apart. When set in this manner, every other row is blanched by setting up boards, running lengthwise, on each side of the row. The same method may be followed with the intervening rows, or they can be banked with earth after the first have been blanched and gone to market. Celery blanched with boards is more easily cleaned for the table or market, but the process is less efficient as a means of inducing crisp and tender growths. Paris Golden is also known as (Golden) Self-Blanching, and the designation is true, to a certain extent, owing to its close habit and compact, erect manner of growth. This shapely style of growth, and also the clear golden-yellow color of the hearts, and of the leaves, after the blanching process has been applied, contribute to make it a very attractive kind. It is a sort very easily grown; it shows well when put up for market; keeps well in the boxes, and looks well on the table; — but it is not first class in quality. However, for early use, large quantities are disposed of, and the thing that will sell is the thing to grow. It is usually sold from the field, being a sort that does not keep well in pits; and lasts till after Thanksgiving.

White Plume, already spoken of, is attractive looking in growth, and also when prepared for market is very handsome; and is of excellent quality. This sort is blanched by banking with earth until ready for market; like Paris Golden, it is best sold directly from the field. The inner stalks and leaves of this variety are naturally white.

Giant Pascal is a new sort, a sport from Paris Golden. It is already becoming quite popular, and for keeping it is one of the best varieties grown; it is of good quality and can be kept quite late. The blanching is done in the field by banking with earth. To insure its keeping, it must be dug in a very short time after the banking; and the banking must be done quite late if it is to be kept for winter use.

The Arlington is an established favorite — a very sure-growing celery, and for early and late is one of the best; while for the garden where only a few are grown it is the best of all. It is blanched by banking with earth. For late keeping, bank a short time before putting into pits. When ripe, this is one of the best eating varieties.

Boston Market is the oldest of all, and when properly grown is still best of all. It is very liable to blight unless grown on moist land; it will keep longest of any, but all depends on it being grown well.

For profit, the Paris Golden and Arlington will do best. The Pascal can be grown six inches apart in the row, six feet between rows; the Arlington and Boston Market the same, by the latest practice.

The market now demands a bunch of solid hearts; this is made by putting two or three together. Preparing the celery for market is laborious and expensive — the most expensive stage through which it passes. Every separate root has to be dug, trimmed, knifed, washed, and packed. Sometimes two or even three roots are required to make a bunch equivalent to one good-sized root; and ten dozen bunches, even after the digging and bringing into the shed, will, in being prepared for market, make a large day's work for one man; the usual average being from six to eight dozen in a day of eleven or twelve hours. It is usually packed in boxes of three dozen in each; but the Arlington will almost always fill with two and one-half dozen. It cannot be grown (counting every root) for less than four cents per root, and leave any profit to the grower. It is sold by market-gardeners at wholesale, by the box of two and one-half or three dozen, the price varying from one dollar to six dollars.

CHICORY (*Chicorium Intybus*) is generally grown for the roots, which are used for adulterating coffee; but sometimes the plants, when about a foot high, are tied together at the top, and then earthed up to bleach, like celery. When so treated they make a good salad. The seed should be sown early in the spring, in drills fifteen or eighteen inches apart, and half an inch deep. The plants when well up should be thinned to six or eight inches. It is a poor crop to introduce on a farm, or in a garden, for if allowed to go to seed, it will spread all over the place.

CHIVES (*Allium Schœnoprasum*) are a small, bulbous-rooted variety of the Onion family; entirely hardy in any part of the United States. Of late years they are less grown than formerly. Then, no family garden was considered properly stocked without a few bunches of Chives. They require no culture beyond keeping the ground free from weeds, and can be continuously grown on almost any soil year after year without change of location. They are propagated by dividing the root, like Pie Plant, or Rhubarb, and the sets should be put in at ten or twelve inches apart. The leaves or stalks are the edible portion, and may be repeatedly cut off, as they continually renew themselves during the growing season. Sometimes they are used in soups, for flavoring; but more commonly in the raw state, for garnishing. In old-time gardens, Chives were often set out as borders for vegetable beds, as they needed no renewing, and their bright green color was quite ornamental.

Field Corn—Traced Ears.

CHAPTER V.

VEGETABLES, ETC. — CONTINUED.

CORN (*Zea Mays*). The COMMON FIELD sort is not a market garden crop: yet we cannot leave wholly unmentioned this, the "king crop of the country." The cheap and easily tilled lands of the great West, with the labor-saving machinery lately brought into use, furnish this corn at such low prices that many farmers prefer to buy their supply rather than grow it. But, where there is suitable land that is not too valuable, it is, in our opinion, cheaper in the long run for the owner to grow his home supply.

The soil best adapted to corn is what is generally called "warm" land; that is, a rather light sandy or gravelly loam with a porous sub-soil, well enriched and thoroughly worked.

There is no crop which will respond more quickly to careful and liberal treatment, as is proven by the fact that, within the last few years, so large a yield as 240 bushels of ears has been produced on a single acre; and this was in the Eastern States, where — so our Western neighbors claim — we have no good land. This is, of course, only a single instance, and the large crop was obtained by exceptionally careful culture.

In the Middle States, or in southern localities, it is well to get northern grown seed ; which, if carefully selected, is sure to be earlier. Within the past few years some marked improvements have been made in varieties of field corn, which will. no doubt, prove permanent acquisitions; but farmers should not put too much confidence in novelties.

SWEET CORN, also, — unless when grown expressly for extra early marketing, — is too little profitable for a garden crop, and in fact is very little grown by gardeners. The principal sort raised in this vicinity is the Extra Early Crosby, — that being the earliest of all. A strong, sandy loam is its favorite soil. It should be planted, for the early crop, about the first of May. Sow in rows four feet apart, and hills three or four feet apart in the row, according to the condition of the soil. It is usually manured in the hill (besides the broadcasting) with one or two shovelfuls of well-rotted manure. The corn is planted by hand ; and, in early planting, should be covered not over one inch deep. Later plantings should be put in deeper. At thinning time four plants should be left in each hill. Clean culture should be given, and the earth should be drawn slightly towards the hills so that water will not stand about the stalks.

If the season should prove favorable, the early crop should be ready for marketing about July 15th. At this date there would be little corn in the market except that brought from the South, and the ears should bring from twenty-five to thirty cents per dozen. At this price the crop from an acre would

SWEET CORN — BEST VARIETIES.   127

bring from $300 to $350. If the Extra Early Crosby is grown, the whole crop may be harvested at two pickings, and marketed before other sorts come in to any ex-

Crosby's Extra Early.   Mammoth.   Early Marblehead.

tent. As an additional advantage the land is cleared in time for a second cropping. The true early variety does not grow over three and a half or four feet high.

The Early Crosby (an older variety) is a favorite with many growers and private gardeners as a medium early sort.

Ruby, a new medium early variety, is likely to become a very decided favorite. The stalk, and also the

Ruby Sweet Corn.

husk, are of a ruby red color; the kernel is very white, of good size, and excellent flavor. It is a twelve-rowed sort: very prolific.

Early Marblehead is by some, wrongly, considered the first and earliest variety, and is raised to some extent; it has a short stalk, bearing ears of fair market size, well filled with plump kernels, and very sweet; but the red color of the cob is a most decided objection to it in some markets. The same objection applies to the Early Narragansett, which before the introduction of the Marblehead was thought by many to lead all in earliness.

Early Minnesota is a familiar variety, much esteemed for the home garden, where a few days in earliness is of less importance than ears of good size and quality. Black Mexican is an eight-rowed variety, having ears of medium size. For quality and real sugary flavor it is unexcelled by any variety in cultivation; but to some the black color of the kernels is uninviting.

The Moore's Concord is a twelve to sixteen-rowed sort, not raised by market-gardeners, because it is so late that by the time it is ready for picking the market is flooded. No one can afford to raise it except farmers who have an abundance of land, and to whom the stover is of as much value as the ears. The quality of this variety is most excellent, and the ears are large. Marblehead Mammoth is a first-rate large-eared variety, twelve to eighteen-rowed, of vigorous growth and excellent quality; cob white, large and well filled; very productive and fine-flavored, the largest and latest of all. Stowell's Evergreen is yet another late standard sort, twelve to sixteen-rowed, very sweet and of good quality; keeps in a green state longer than any other kind.

CORN SALAD (*Valerianella olitoria*), or Fetticus, is a peculiar vegetable, used entirely as a salad. In England it is largely grown. Some years ago it was very frequently raised among growing corn, but it is now considered better to give the crop full possession of the land. It is but little grown for the Boston market, but in New York there is quite a demand for it. It should be sown as early in the spring as the ground can be worked, in rows twelve or fifteen inches apart. If the weather is favorable, it should be ready for use in about two months from the date of sowing. When an early spring supply is to be provided for, it may be sown about the middle of September. The plants should receive a covering of straw, or marsh hay, as soon as cold weather comes. They start very early in the spring, and therefore the covering should be removed in March or early April. The further treatment and marketing are the same as with spinach.

CRESS (*Lepidium sativum*), or Peppergrass, is in some respects like Corn Salad. The culture is very simple. Sow in early spring, in rows twelve or fifteen inches apart. Make a sowing every ten or fifteen days, as it runs very quickly to seed. The leaves, when young, have a pungent taste and are used as a salad, and also for garnishing. The Curled is the best for general use, although several other varieties are cultivated.

UPLAND CRESS (*Barbarea vulgaris*) is classed as a separate vegetable, being different from the common Curled Cress both as regards parentage and habit of growth — though similarly used as a small salad. It is a hardy perennial, thriving on any soil, wet or dry. It makes an early appearance in spring, and grows with such extraordinary rapidity that in a few days it may be gathered for use; weeks ahead of any other out-door growths. It is as easy of culture as spinach, can be grown easily for two years without re-sowing, and yields enormous crops. The seed should be sown in April.

CUCUMBER (*Cucumis sativus*).— While this is a very important out-door crop, it is also very extensively grown under glass, for the Boston market; and cultivated in this manner (as a forced crop) it is probably dealt in to a larger extent here than in any other market of the United States. Almost every market-gardener in this section who has any glass runs it, either early or late, to cucumbers. As is well known, the plant is a very tender one when grown out-doors, and when forced under glass is much more so.

The seed for the first crop is generally sown about the middle of March. When the plants are sufficiently grown they are transplanted, being set four in a hill; and thirty-two hills being put under each 3 x 6 sash. They are left to grow in this manner until they are about four inches high (which usually takes about four weeks from the time of sowing). They are then removed; and each hill is placed under a 3 x 6 sash, and given good, steady heat, such as keeps the ground and roots thoroughly warm. The bed should be kept at an average temperature of about 70°, corresponding to ordinary midsummer weather. The requisite heat is afforded by the heating material that has been placed underneath, aided by the sun, and is retained at night by covering with mats and shutters. It is regulated by means of a thermometer, and ought not to run lower than 50° at night, or higher than 90° during the day. In case the thermometer rises higher than this, the beds should be cooled by raising the sash. The vines are sometimes grown in lettuce beds, after the lettuce has been removed, by putting in fresh heating material, but it is much better, when practicable, to make a fresh bed. The plants, after being established, should be reduced to three in a hill, as it is no advantage, but a drawback, to have too much vine. They require the same care under glass that they would receive in field culture. Especially under glass they are a very quick-growing crop, and will require picking as often as four times a week. The picking may ordinarily be commenced about June 1st; and about this time the glass should be removed from the bed. Those gathered in the earliest pickings usually bring about ten cents each; of course as the season advances the price will decrease, but a hill started at the time stated should bring about $4.00; and later plantings less, according to the season and the supply. The early beds usually continue in bearing until about July 15th, or between six or seven weeks.

There are very few that raise an acre of cucumbers under glass; but where they do, their receipts ought to be, as a fair average result, not less than $3,000.

The plan above described is that followed by most growers, and involves less risk than in houses; but by the method of house-culture cucumbers may be grown at any time during the season. Where crops are to be grown for continuous supply during the winter, the first sowing is done early in September. Vines of this sowing will come into bearing about Christmas; and at that season of the year cucumbers will usually bring from forty to fifty cents each. Although this is a large price, growing and selling them in this way is not very profitable; it is attended with much risk and uncertainty, and the crops are always very light. The vines are left to bear as long as they continue doing well. Then the ground is cleared off, and another sowing is made, say in January, and its product is ready for picking in April. In the houses the vines are not allowed to rest on the ground, as they do in the beds, but are trained on trellises of various styles. Thus the cucumbers may be seen with all facility during growth, and taken when ready for picking. Where cucumbers are grown exclusively in the houses, only two crops can be raised each winter.

For the first early out-door crop the plants should be started under glass about five weeks before they are wanted for transplanting. Thirty-two hills are started under each 3 x 6 sash; and when the fourth leaf is well out the hills are transplanted to the field. The roots can be saved from disturbance by using a piece of stove-pipe eight inches in diameter and six high, to cut down around each hill; the shovel being then thrust under, and the plants thus enclosed and supported during removal. Where sods can be obtained to plant in they are often used, for convenience in handling; but the supply is apt to be deficient. The rows should be six feet apart; hills four feet apart in the row, and slightly elevated so that water cannot settle on them.

At first a close watch should be kept for bugs: plaster or other dust will be effectual in repelling them. Cultivate as for any out-door crop. In the bearing season the cucumbers will generally bring from one to two cents a piece; and the entire crop of an acre, at this price, will amount to $400 or $500. On high-priced land the entire crop should be marketed for the table, as growing for the pickle factories cannot be made to pay. For pickles, the seed may be put in at any time from the middle of June to the 20th of July. They may be planted as close as four feet apart, each way. The pickles are sold by the thousand, at prices which vary greatly.

Among varieties the White Spine is the leading table sort grown for this market, both out-doors and under glass. Rawson's Improved is the best strain on the market, and this I use exclusively, in forcing and in

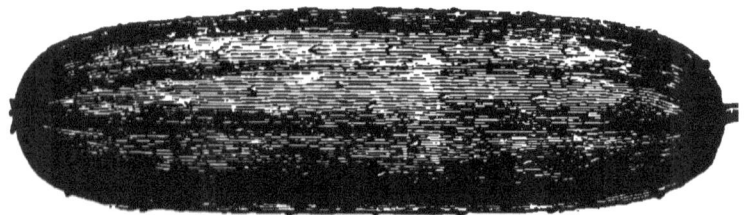

Rawson's White Spine Cucumber.

out-door culture, for table use. It grows very even in size — crisp and good. The Early Cluster is a very popular early variety, which produces cucumbers in clusters. The Green Prolific, a pickling variety, favored by many, has a similar habit of growth. The Boston Pickling is considered the leading pickling variety, and is a heavy yielder. The Long Green is a well-known late variety, grown here to some extent for family use — more largely in England. The Extra Early Russian is an odd-looking, netted variety, very early.

DANDELION (*Leontodon Taraxacum*) is almost exclusively a Boston market crop. In this vicinity, the demand is such that it is grown by the acre; and, although there is no demand for it at present in other large markets, yet (as the consumption here is steadily increasing) it may be safely inferred that its use, like that of celery, is likely to become more general. It in some respects resembles endive, and certainly is one of the most healthful of all spring greens.

Dandelion.

It should be sown in drills as early in the spring as the ground can be worked. Although it is a very hardy plant, the seed must have very careful treatment in order to obtain a good stand, and should be covered not over one-fourth of an inch deep. The ground should then be made firm, so as to retain the moisture. In this section they succeed best on a rather light, sandy soil. It does not need to be very rich, or heavily manured. For field culture, the rows should be put one foot apart. The dandelions, when they first come up, are so dark colored as to be almost invisible. A little lettuce seed, say one ounce per acre, mixed and sown with the dandelion, will come up quickly and show the rows plainly. When sown in beds, to be forced, the rows should be six inches apart. Roots may be removed from the field to a hot-bed, and forced; but in any case it takes somewhat over a year from the time of sowing to grow the crop. It is marketed precisely as spinach — thirteen pounds weight is considered a bushel. The price varies greatly. On the forced crop from $1.00 to $2.00 is about the range of price. On the out-door crop, $1.00 is considered high, the usual average being lower, and prices sometimes very low. At fifty cents per bushel, the crop is a paying one. When prices run high the proceeds per acre often reach as high as $1,000.

There happens a failure sometimes in starting a crop. The sowing may be renewed any time before the first of August, and provided it comes up well, and escapes scorching by the sun, the crop will be just as early as one sown in April.

Women and boys are usually employed to gather and trim the plants, and remove a portion of the roots before sending to market; at a cost of about 10 cts. per bushel. The roots are often dried, and in this condition are an article of commerce, being used quite extensively for medicinal purposes, and in the manufacture of beer; and also as a substitute for coffee.

The Improved French Thick-Leaved is a great improvement over the common variety; and this is now grown almost exclusively. It is a very vigorous grower, and affords a heavy yield of broad, thick leaves.

EGG PLANT (*Solanum Melongena*). The seed should be sown about March 15th, either in hot-bed or hot-house, the temperature being kept between 60° and 80°.

After the plants have reached a height of three or four inches, they should be transplanted to four inches apart; and after they have made a stocky growth, to such size as to cover the ground, they should be again transplanted to eight inches apart. Then they may stand, and be gradually hardened off until it is time for setting in the open ground.

The ground should be thoroughly prepared, and well enriched, as they are rank feeders; they also require a good deal of moisture. They should be set in rows four feet apart, — plants three feet apart in the row. The New York Purple is the principal variety grown. Black Pekin is earlier and hardier, but not quite so large or fine-looking. Early Long Purple is an oblong-fruited, early variety, of good quality. The fruit varies somewhat in color, from a very dark purple to a lighter shade streaked with yellow.

ENDIVE (*Cichorium Endivia*) is quite a rarity here; but it may soon become quite a popular salad. In New York and Philadelphia there is quite a demand for it.

Endive requires a good supply of moisture, and should be sown where it will be least exposed to heat and drought. As it is used principally during the fall months, the main sowings are usually made in June or July, in properly prepared beds, and the plants, after they have reached the proper height, are transplanted to rows two feet apart, with plants at intervals of six inches in the row.

They have to be blanched by gathering up the leaves and tying them together at the top with bass matting, and in a month or six weeks' time (varying according to the season), the plants will be ready for use.

The Green Curled is very hardy, and blanched easily. It is also largely used for garnishing.

The Moss Curled is a newer variety, and somewhat larger. It makes a most excellent salad, and is also very ornamental. The Broad-Leaved Batavian is used to some extent, principally for soups, but is not nearly as good as the curled varieties.

HERBS (*Culinary, Sweet, or Medicinal*) constitute a class of garden products, of which some mention should be made here. It may be remarked that Herbs in general love a mellow and free soil; also, that care should be taken to harvest them properly, and without exposure to wet. Selecting a suitable day, cut them when lacking a little of being in full blossom, and dry them quickly in the shade in a secure place; after which pack them close in dry boxes or vessels, and keep them entirely excluded from the air. So treated, they can be kept on hand without deterioration until they can be sold to advantage. Still, only a few are raised, though the list is a long one. We select for description a few of the more prominent kinds.

Anise (*Pimpinella anisum*) is a native of Asia Minor Greece, and Egypt. The seeds are used in medicine, also in the manufacture of liquors, and in some parts of Europe as a spice for cooking purposes. Sow in April or May in a warm, rich soil, in a permanent location.

Balm (*Melissa officinalis*). This plant is a native of Southern Europe. It is used for seasoning, and in the manufacture of certain perfumes. Sow in a warm location, preferably in a deep, sandy loam; though the plant will succeed almost anywhere.

Basil, Sweet (*Ocymum basilicum*) is a native of India. The leaves are used for seasoning, and, to a limited extent, for medicinal purposes. Sow in hotbed, or green-house, if practicable, in March or April, and transplant to open ground after the weather is settled. A sandy soil is almost essential.

Caraway (*Carum carvi*). A native of Europe, produces the "caraway seed" which is so universally used for flavoring. The plant is of the easiest possible culture, no care being necessary, but simply to scatter the seed where the growth is wanted.

Lavender (*Lavendula vera*) is a native of Southern Europe; known everywhere, and largely grown in certain parts of Europe for the oil, which is distilled from the flowers, and is used in perfumes. The plant is also quite ornamental and is worthy of cultivation on this account alone. Choose, if possible, a deep, mellow soil.

Marjoram, Sweet (*Origanum marjoram*). This plant is probably a native of Portugal, though found in other countries of Southern Europe. It is grown entirely for seasoning or flavoring purposes; the leaves and the ends of the shoots being the parts used. Sow early in the spring in any good soil.

ROSEMARY (*Rosemarinus officinalis*) is a native of Southern Europe. Its leaves, when dried, are used for

Rosemary.

seasoning. The plants may be grown from seed, but the easier mode of propagation is by division of the roots. A warm location should be chosen.

SAGE, COMMON (*Salvia officinalis*) is also a native of Southern Europe. The uses to which this herb is put are numerous, and too well known to be enumerated. Sow in spring wherever desired, and thin to six or eight inches apart in the row. A well-drained soil is essential. Give clean culture.

SUMMER SAVORY (*Satureja hortensis*). Native of Europe. This is one of the most common of cultivated herbs. The leaves and tender leaf-stalks are used for flavoring, and especially when cooked with beans impart a very pleasant flavor. The seed may be sown in open ground in early spring; or, if desired, the plants may be started under glass. A light, rich soil should be selected.

TANSY (*Tanacetum vulgare*) is cultivated in gardens and also found as a roadside weed; growing from two to four feet in height, with smooth, strong-scented foliage of acrid taste. *T. balsamita* is smaller, sweet-scented, with pale yellow flowers.

THYME (*Thymus vulgaris*) is a native of Southern Europe. The leaves and young shoots are used for seasoning. The plants may be propagated either from seeds or cuttings, the former being preferable. Sow in early spring, and in midsummer transplant to five or six inches apart in the row or border.

HORSERADISH (*Cochlearia Armoracia*) is raised from sets saved during preparation for market of the previous crop. These are put into the ground as early as the soil can be prepared. Plough four furrows together, and thus form a ridge; along the middle of this ridge the sets are planted by hand, eighteen inches apart, and covered two inches deep. A series of ridges thus formed will bring the rows about three and one-half feet apart. A row of spinach is sown on one side of this ridge, and a row of beets on the other side, leaving the centre occupied by the horseradish, which is very slow in starting, so that the others will not interfere with it at all. The spinach is cut off early; and the beets, after they have made a proper growth, are thinned for greens, while those that are left to grow are soon gathered and bunched for early marketing. By this time the horseradish will have reached a height of five or six inches, and can now be hoed and cultivated.

Before being marketed for grating, it is washed by putting it in tubs of water and stirring and brushing with a broom. It is then usually packed in barrels.

For bunching, more pains must be taken, and the washing must be a more thorough one; after which it is tied up in bundles of five or six pounds each, and in this way brings a little extra price. By the barrel it usually brings from 5 to 6 cents per pound; each barrelful weighing about one hundred pounds.

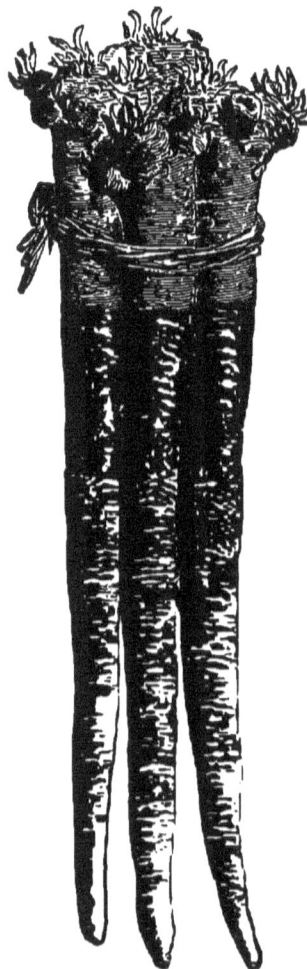
Horse Radish.

At the foregoing price, an acre of horseradish, if it succeeded well, would bring a return of about $350. Adding for the spinach and beets, the total product should amount to about $600 per acre for the year.

Kohl Rabi (*Brassica caulo-rapa*) in some respects resembles turnip, but is actually a variety of the cabbage; the bulb is really an enlarged stem, of a fleshy, pulpy consistency. Its shape is that of an almost regular ball; in some varieties about as large as an average sized orange, while in others it is nearly as large as a man's head. In flavor it closely resembles the turnip, and partly also the cabbage, blending the two.  It is highly appreciated in New York, especially amongst the Germans. It is in its best condition for use before it becomes fully grown, even while quite small; and is prepared for the table in the same manner as turnips. The seed-bed should be made in May or June. Transplant to rows three feet apart, fifteen inches apart in the row.

The crop is fitted for market by bunching when green and tender; three bulbs being put in a bunch. The price obtained varies from seventy-five cents to one dollar per dozen bunches. Any that are left unsold may be used for stock feeding. They are often grown expressly for that object. They may be kept as easily as turnips, and the method of storing is the same. The Early White Vienna is the leading variety. It is in the best condition for the table when as large as an ordinary cocoanut. It is then tender and of fine flavor, but later on becomes tough, stringy, and unpalatable.

Early Purple Vienna closely resembles the preceding, except that the color of the bulb is deep purple instead of greenish white. There is but little choice between the two. The Giant White is larger and coarser, and the Goliath is truly a mammoth kind: these are raised only for stock.

LEEK (*Allium porrum*) is a hardy biennial plant,

London Flag Leek.

producing an oblong bulb, or stalk, which has the flavor of an onion, and is used principally for flavoring soups and stews. It is useless to attempt its cultivation on light, poor land. Sow the seed early in May, in a well prepared bed, and transplant in July to rows three feet apart, putting two plants to each foot of row, on land from which a crop of cabbage or lettuce has been removed. Set them rather deep, and in cultivating draw up the earth, so as to bleach them slightly and keep them tender.

The Leek is used principally during the winter months, and may be stored in trenches, in the same manner as celery; or it may be placed in a cool cellar, with the roots resting on a layer of soil. In this way, if standing thickly together, they will take root slightly, and keep very fresh and green until late the following spring.

The Musselburgh is the principal market variety, although the London Flag closely resembles it and is just as good. The Giant Carentan is a newer sort, large and of good quality, and will, no doubt, prove quite popular.

LETTUCE (*Lactuca sativa*). This is one of the leading crops, and is perhaps the most profitable one raised by market gardeners. It is the only vegetable that is continuously grown throughout the year, being produced under glass in hot-houses, or hot-beds, in winter, and in the open ground in the summer.

For forcing in hot-houses, seed is sown for plants of the first setting about the first of September, in the open ground; these are afterwards transplanted into the houses. The resulting crop is ready for marketing about the middle of November. Sowings are made about ten days apart, from time to time, throughout the season, so as to give a continuous supply of plants. Lettuce seed is very small, and when sown under glass requires but little covering. One ounce of good seed is sufficient for four sashes of the ordinary size, three feet by six.

The culture of Lettuce as an out-door crop is comparatively easy; but when grown under glass it is a much more difficult crop to raise, as through the winter season, when the days are short and there is much cloudy weather, the crop is likely to be affected with mildew and the green-fly.

This green-fly, or louse, is a most difficult insect to manage, especially when the plants have gained a considerable size. The only way to keep rid of them is to fumigate the houses thoroughly with the smoke of tobacco stems. This should be done three nights in succession. In order to make sure of accomplishing the work, in a week or ten days after the third smoking the operation should be repeated; and by this process, if carefully and thoroughly carried out at the proper times, a crop already attacked may be saved; but it requires thorough treatment. The tobacco stems should be moistened before being used, or the heat will be too much for the lettuce. Some skill and discretion are necessary to determine just how much to moisten them, and how to do the smoking in the proper manner. On these points a practical experience is the very best possible teacher, although somewhat costly at times. After the first of February there is but very little trouble with this insect.*

* Consult Chapter VII.

After the plants have been treated in this manner they will be ready for transplanting into beds or wherever required; while if this treatment should not be given them, it is quite likely they might be destroyed. Occasionally, it is true, these insects do not trouble a crop at all; but it is much the best policy to be on the safe side and use every precaution.

Through damp and cloudy weather the plants are liable to mildew, both in the houses and in frames. Although not as troublesome as insects, mildew often destroys a crop. This can be avoided by keeping up as high a temperature as possible, while still giving plenty of air.

In transplanting lettuce, the plants should at first be put four inches apart, and when they have covered the ground should be moved to eight inches apart in the houses.

In hot-beds, fifty plants are put under each 3x6 sash, which makes the distances separating the plants about seven and a half inches each way.

The price for lettuce, through the winter, averages about four cents per single head, or fifty cents per dozen. Three crops can be grown in the hot-houses during the winter. Three can be taken from the hot-beds also, if the plants are started in the houses and grown there until the last transplanting.

The heat for hot-beds, as has been before said, is mostly horse manure fresh from the stable; and it takes one cord of this for every eight sash for the early or winter beds; but for those started after the fifteenth of February one cord will answer for twelve

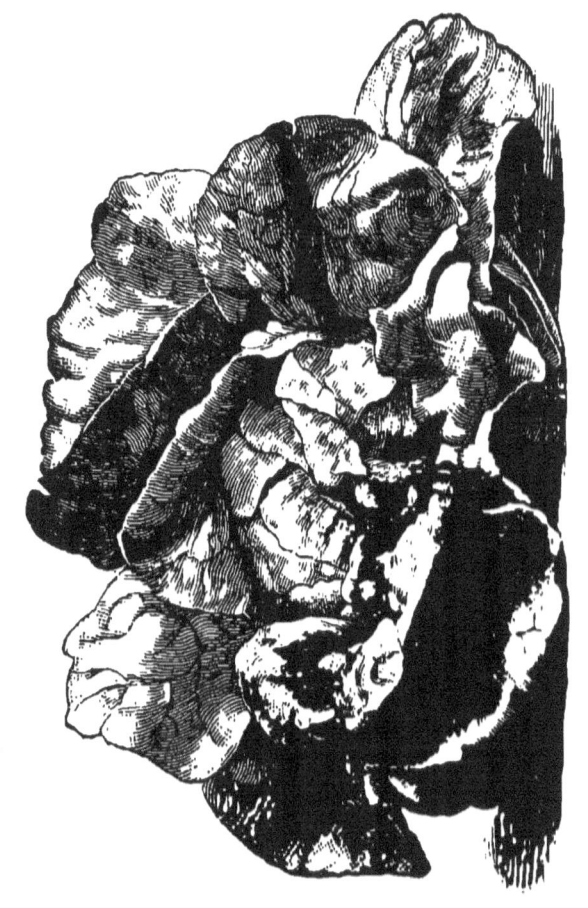

Rawson's New Hot-House Lettuce.

sash. The expense of this, all put into the bed and ready for use, is nearly one dollar per sash, reckoning the putting down of bed, putting on sash, mats, and shutters, and bed set out to lettuce; so that the cost of raising lettuce in the winter with four dozen under each sash is twenty-five cents per dozen to start with; add cost of the plants, twelve cents per dozen, and taking care of them twelve cents more; making the cost of raising lettuce in the winter season fifty cents per dozen, without reckoning in the carrying to market.

The second crop can be grown much cheaper than the first, say at forty cents per dozen; because the bed is all ready. It will require only two-thirds as much manure; and not over two-thirds as much time will be consumed in taking care of the second crop as of the first. Then, too, the spent manure that is taken out in renewing the beds is worth something, perhaps all of half price, or we may say twenty-five cents per sash, for use elsewhere. But, allowing for all this, I believe there is no profit from growing lettuce in hot-beds at fifty cents per dozen. In houses it can be grown for less than in beds, and its cultivation in houses is thought to pay fairly well.

The temperature in the houses should be kept between 40° and 45° in the night time, and at from 60° to 70° during the day. That of the hot-beds also should be regulated in a similar manner.

In this vicinity the White-Seeded Tennis-ball has been almost exclusively the variety raised for forcing; but the Black-Seeded is preferred for out-door culture, the latter being much larger than the former.

Another sort, Rawson's New Hot-house, is now fast taking the place of the White-Seeded Tennis-ball for forcing. It is nearly double the size of the latter variety, and exhibits qualities of most superior excellence. The cut shown on page 148 is a correct likeness, having been taken from a photograph. This kind is altogether the best yet introduced for growing in greenhouses and hot-beds; being the largest lettuce grown, and being also a sure header; and not liable to rot in the heart. These important traits make it an extremely desirable sort, and profitable in cultivation.

As we have remarked, the first sowing of seed for plants to be forced is made about September 1st. Black-Seeded Tennis-ball is first sown in February, in the houses; and then transplanted to hot-beds. After being hardened off, it is set in the open ground about the last of April or the first of May, and will be fit for cutting about the first of June. The price for this lettuce is about the same as for that grown in the houses. This is set, in the field, about one foot apart; or it may be set among cabbage; or in the onion field, where space has been left for a later growth of celery. As soon as the ground can be worked in the spring, a sowing of the Black-Seeded variety is made in the open ground; the rows being spaced one foot apart, and every other row being left out so that celery may be set in later. When the plants are large enough, they are thinned so as to stand one foot apart in the row.

Sowings are made in this way every ten days until about the twentieth of August. These sowings, taken with those made under glass, as described, give continuously maturing crops of lettuce the year round.

Early Curled Silesia is a very early curled sort, used extensively for first early out-door crops.

Next after the forcing and early out-door lettuces comes the Boston Fine Curled; which may either be forced under glass or grown in out-door culture. Early Curled Simpson is another excellent curled variety, pale green in color. It does not form very compact heads. Hanson is one of the leading "head" lettuces for house, garden and other out-door culture.

The name "Cos" applied to lettuce denotes a class of plants distinguished by the formation of tall upright-growing leaves without disposition to head — a defect supplied by the art of the grower, who gathers these leaves together and binds them into a compact bunch or head; when they blanch and grow tender, thus becoming fit in their appearance and condition for market and for the table.

Bath Cos Lettuce.

White Paris Cos is the best of the Cos varieties. It is a quick grower, and has been rapidly gaining in ularity for the past few years. The Bath Cos is crisp and fine flavored, and extremely large.

The Green Curled is an exceedingly ornamental, fringed variety, and is rapidly gaining in favor in family gardens.

There is an almost endless list of varieties, but none are more desirable than those above mentioned.

MARTYNIA (*Martynia*). The young seed pods of this plant are used to some extent for pickling. It is of very easy culture, and will succeed in almost any garden soil.

The seed may be sown in the hot-bed, — the plants being afterwards transplanted, — or may be sown in April in the open ground, and transplanted later. They should be spaced to three feet apart each way, as the plants are very spreading in habit.

Martynia.

On good soil the pods are produced in great abundance, and should be ready for use in July or August.

MUSHROOMS (*Agaricus Campestris*). This is a very peculiar crop, and one that is found in many respects quite difficult to grow. The best plan is as follows: Take fresh horse manure and shake out all the straw and coarse part, using nothing but the fine portion of it. Mix this with fresh loam, one part loam to two parts manure, and turn the pile every day to keep it from burning, until the fiery heat is nearly all out of it. Construct the bed about four feet wide and as long as required, putting in the prepared material about eight inches deep, and making it very solid as it is put

Mushroom Beds.

in. Let it remain in this condition, until the temperature has become reduced to 90°; then make holes two or three inches deep, at a distance of twelve inches apart each way, into which put the spawn in pieces about as large as a hen's egg. Cover the spawn and let it remain undisturbed for eight or ten days; then cover the whole bed with fine loam, to the depth of two inches, making it firm with the back of a shovel or spade. Apply water only when the soil is very dry.

The bed must be in a covered situation, and in a dark place, with the temperature at about 50°, and the prepared soil must be kept dry from the commencement. If everything favors, the mushrooms will appear in six or eight weeks, and will continue over two months. By careful applications of water at the temperature of about 70° the season may be prolonged.

MUSKMELON (*Cucumis melo*). The Muskmelon will succeed best in soil naturally strong and rich, and on a recently turned sod. The best way is to turn the land over at the proper time and apply about five cords of manure broadcast, using a spreader where one can be had. After harrowing thoroughly the ground should be marked off for hills, six feet apart each way. A shovelful of fine manure should be applied in the hills, which should be slightly raised, so that water will not stand around the plants. Seven or eight seeds should be put in a hill so as to make allowance for insects. The planting may be done about May 15th.

After the plants have got their fourth leaf well out, and have obtained a good start, they should be thinned to three in a hill. Cultivate both ways thoroughly, the same as a crop of squash or other vines would be treated. They should never be hoed or worked around when the leaves are wet with rain or dew.

In picking for market, it is an easy matter to tell when the fruit is fit to be taken, as the under side of the melon will be lightly streaked with yellow. If picked then and exposed to the sun for a couple of days, they will be ready for the table of the consumer.

They are rather an uncertain crop, and are cultivated but very little by market-gardeners in this section.

The melons of this class are all yellow-fleshed. There are several varieties; but the Arlington Long Yellow is almost exclusively the one here raised for market. In shape it is oblong, with a skin thickly netted, flesh thick and of fine flavor.

Another variety, which is claimed to be very distinct, highly productive, and one likely to become very popular with melon-growers, is the Osage. It is of western origin and not yet well known here; so that we do not undertake to decide on its merits. Its skin is said to be very thin, of dark-green color, and slightly netted; seed cavity very small; flesh of a salmon color, extremely sweet, and possessing a peculiar spicy flavor; very thick, and good through to the rind. It is, moreover, said to be a good keeper and to stand shipping better than any other variety known. This description affords a pretty complete list of everything we know of that is wanted in a muskmelon.

Cantaloupe is our name for round kinds. These are usually started about May 1st, under glass, to be transplanted, about June 10th, to the open field. The bed is usually placed near the centre of the field where they are to be grown, and the seed is started on sods 9 inch by 9 inch, so that thirty-two hills are started under each 3 x 6 sash.

The Arlington Nutmeg is the leading first early variety, and is followed by the Hackensack, which is

Cantaloupes.

one of the most popular sorts for the main crop. The latter is of good size and of excellent quality.

The Casaba is a large, late variety, and in the Northern States always requires to be started under glass in order to give it time to ripen its fruit before frost.

The Surprise is a variety of rather recent introduction and of considerable merit for the home garden but it is not large enough for market.

White Japan is quite a popular sort, of most excellent quality. It is of medium size, with skin pale yellow in color, while the flesh is golden.

Montreal Market is the largest melon of its class in cultivation, and derives its name from being originated and largely grown in the vicinity of Montreal. This is started under glass, earlier than the others, and is grown almost invariably in the beds until the time of picking. It is a very thick-meated, green-fleshed sort, and is considered the best sort, for table use, in existence. Good specimens of its fruit, well grown and ripened, often bring as high as $1.00 each, at wholesale. As they produce more vines than the other varieties they must be given more room. Where one hill is planted under a sash the beds should be set so that the hills will be twelve feet apart the other way. One plant per hill, at this distance, is sufficient. In picking for market, it has to be noted that the fruit is never ripe until the stem will part readily from it.

MUSTARD (*Sinapis alba* and *nigra*). Used to some extent for greens, early in the spring, but more especially as a salad. It may be sown in the open ground (almost any time after the soil can be properly prepared) in rows twelve inches apart : also may be forced in the hot-bed, or hot-house, and thus may be had at all seasons of the year; but the demand is small.

White Mustard is the variety best liked as a salad; and the seed, which is of a very bright yellow color, affords, when ground, the mustard which we use on our tables. Black-seeded is much like the preceding,

Black Seeded Mustard.

except that the seed is very dark in color and the leaves are a trifle more pungent. It is used both as a salad and for manufacturing into table mustard.

NASTURTIUM (*Tropæolum majus*) is but little grown, either in the market or home garden; but the shoots and flower buds make an excellent salad, and the seeds of the Dwarf variety (*T. minus*) when pickled in vinegar can hardly be distinguished from caper sauce.

It can be easily grown in any garden soil, and will twine around brush, or any other support that may be near. It is sown in drills in early spring, being covered about one inch deep.

A large number of varieties may be found catalogued in the published flower-seed lists; but the Tall and Dwarf are the only kinds grown in the vegetable garden. The former grows to a height of eight or nine feet; and is a first-rate ornamental plant to set for climbing over rock work or on a trellis. The Dwarf never grows above three or three and a half feet in height; and this, when sown in drills, should be bushed like early peas.

OKRA (*Hibiscus esculentus*) is grown for its seed pods, which, when young and tender, are used in soups and stews; but sales in the Boston market are very light. It is of very easy culture, as it succeeds on almost any soil, and after the plants are once up and growing is quite hardy. But the seeds should not be put in till the weather is warm and fairly settled,— say about the 10th of May, — as they are liable to rot if placed in the soil when it is cold and soggy. In this one respect they are very tender, and are found difficult to start except under favorable conditions. There are but two varieties on the list; these are the Tall and Dwarf kinds.

In the culture of either, the planting should be in drills, and the covering two inches deep. If the Dwarf variety is planted at eighteen inches between the drills, it will have space enough; but in cultivating the larger variety, three or three and a half feet will be none too much to leave between the rows. This plant is one which requires nearly the whole season to complete its growth; but, if desired, a few seeds may be started in the hot-bed or hot-house about four weeks before they are wanted for setting out of doors; and in this way they may be hurried forward.

When used in soups, okra imparts a viscous or gummy consistency, and a peculiar flavor which, to most people, is quite agreeable.

Okra.

CHAPTER VI.

Vegetables, Etc. — Continued.

THE ONION (*Allium cepa*) as a paying field crop, ranks next to cabbage. For the early supply, grown for bunching, onion sets are used. These should be planted in rich soil, using from six to ten bushels per acre, according to the size of the sets. Seed is also sown at the same time for plants to follow, and maintain the supply. Six pounds of seed are required for an acre. For raising sets, twenty-five pounds of seed are required, which should be grown on rather poor land, so that they may not run to tops or grow too large.

The White sets are put out in the spring as soon as the ground can be worked, three inches apart, in rows one foot apart, reserving every sixth row for celery. This work is usually done by boys, and the sets are covered in with a rake by a man who follows, walking in the vacant row. Only two weedings will be required; but when seed is sown three are necessary, and the plants are thinned to three inches.

The sets will be large enough for pulling about the middle of June. They are bunched for market, five in

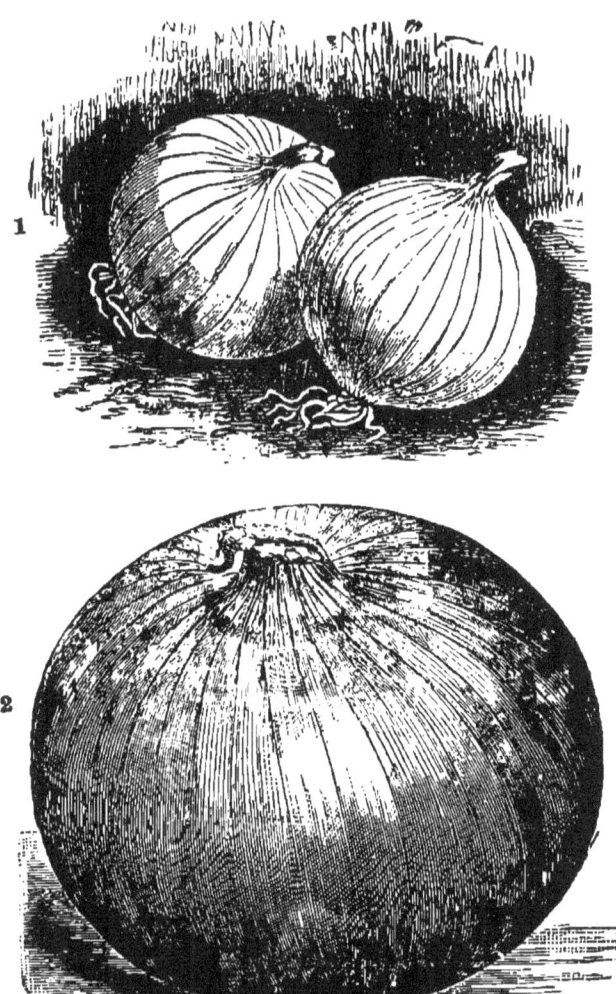

(1) White Portugal. (2) Danvers Thick Yellow.

a bunch at first, and four when they are larger. The pulling continues through July. The price obtained for those first marketed is about sixty cents per dozen bunches, and the average of the whole crop may be from thirty-five to forty cents. The proceeds of an acre should be from $600 to $800, and $300 should cover cost of growing.

Yellow sets do not differ as to culture from the white, but are not used for bunching. Soon after the tops drop over (about July 1st), the onions are pulled up and left to dry on the ground. When they are thoroughly dry the tops are cut off, and the onions are boxed or barreled for sale. The average yield (leaving out the sixth row for celery) is about 500 bushels per acre, and they will bring a price between $1.00 and $1.50 per bushel. In raising late crops for storing, seed is used exclusively, and the plants are thinned to one inch instead of three. These crops are allowed to dry thoroughly in the ground before harvesting. They should be stored in bins or boxes where a steady, cool temperature can be kept up. For fall onions the price obtained is usually about $2.50 per barrel.

Until modern inventions of the labor-saving sort came forward, very largely superseding the old methods of hand-cultivation, the sowing and growing of this valuable and remunerative crop was an extremely tedious and laborious business. Now, after the preparation of the beds has been properly accomplished, a smart boy of sixteen will seed more ground in a day, and do it better, than twenty men could at the time when seed drills were unknown ; and the labor of the after culture during the growth of the plants has been almost equally lightened by modern devices.

The ground must be such as has been well enriched with long and liberal manuring; and recent addition of green manures must not be relied upon for affording the close-growing plants their proper nutrition. The tilth should be as perfect as it can be made, and the plants must have the cleanest possible culture.

The Yellow Danvers, and the White Portugal or Silver Skin, are the kinds grown almost exclusively for this market, from sets and from seeds. In some localities, where red onions are in favor, the Red Wethersfield is highly esteemed. It is a very productive, large sort.

PARSLEY (*Apium petroselinum*) is kept at all seasons

Fine Curled Parsley.

in continuous growth, either under glass or in the open ground. The plants for forcing are kept cut down during the summer, and in the fall are placed under glass at three inches apart, in rows about six inches apart. The pickings may be repeated often during the season, after which the roots are worthless.

The Fine Curled is the variety chiefly grown, and is in fact the most desirable. The Moss Curled though similar, is a little more crimped. Fern-Leaved is an ornamental variety. Plain Parsley is the smooth-leaved sort, used mainly for flavoring. It is hardier, and its leaves are larger and of a deeper green than those of the other sorts named. The average returns, per sash 3 x 6, from forced parsley would be from $3.00 to $4.00.

PARSNIPS (*Pastinaca sativa*) require careful attention to secure proper germination. Thorough preparation of soil and early sowing will promote that result. Sow in rows fifteen inches apart. At this width, an early crop of spinach or radishes may be sown in rows between. These will be out of the way before the parsnips will crowd them. Make the covering not over half an inch deep, and thin to four inches apart. Any convenient part of the crop may be left to stand in the ground over winter (as they are improved by frost), and may be dug for marketing any time after the frost is out. Parsnips will do better (and especially in case they are to remain in the ground over winter) if sown on ridges formed by lapping two furrows together, each ridge planted with two rows. The ridges should be thirty inches apart.

Among varieties, those figured in the cut following are of principal importance. The Short Round French is the earliest, but small in size. Long Smooth is such as its name implies; growing very smooth and true; unsurpassed for market or exhibition, and the

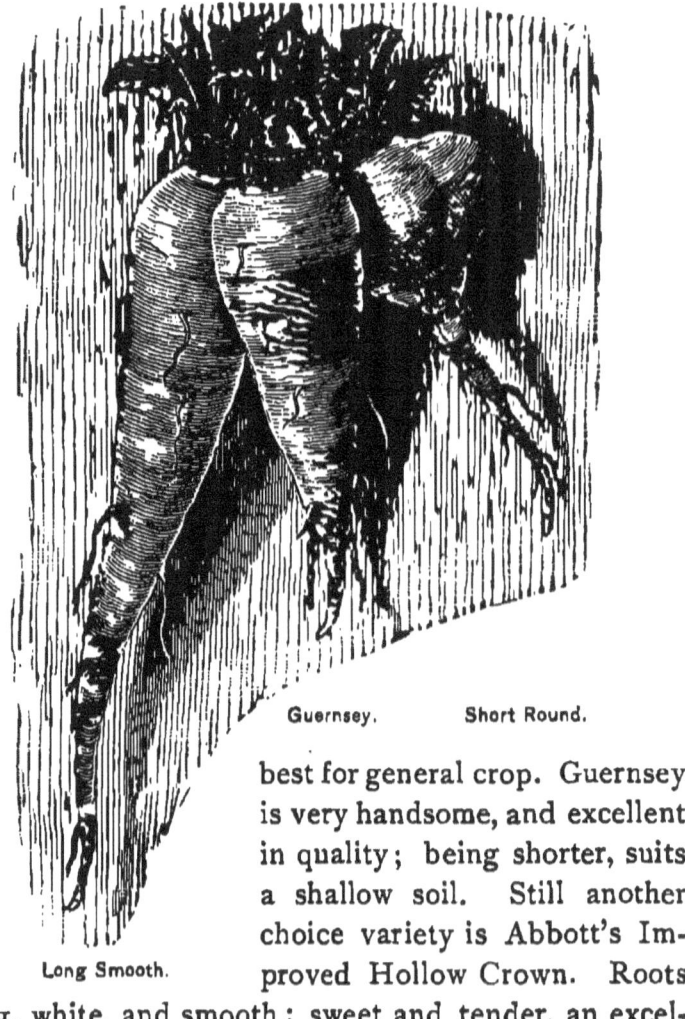

Guernsey.   Short Round.

Long Smooth.

best for general crop. Guernsey is very handsome, and excellent in quality; being shorter, suits a shallow soil. Still another choice variety is Abbott's Improved Hollow Crown. Roots long, white, and smooth; sweet and tender, an excellent sort.

PEAS (*Pisum sativum*), which have been in past years highly profitable, now yield fluctuating and uncertain returns, owing to the shipments of Southern growers. Where cabbage is to follow, the early upright growing sorts are usually sown in three and a half feet rows. Three feet apart does well for American Wonder. When squashes are to follow, two double rows are put in three and a half feet apart, and then a space is reserved about five feet wide, for planting squashes before the peas are ready to be removed.

The Pea comes earliest to maturity in light, rich soil; but for the general crop, a deep loam, or a soil strongly inclining to clay, is the best. Plant as early as the weather will permit, in well prepared ground; cover one inch deep and the seeds will come earlier than if deeper. Later sowings may be covered two to six inches deep; the deep planting tends to prevent mildew; and to prolong the season.

When a sufficient quantity of manure is available, it is always best to manure the peas broadcast before sowing. When manure is applied in this way, the peas will get as much of it as they need, and the balance will remain for the later crop. When it is intended to cultivate in this manner, the early varieties are always sown, as the late ones would not get off soon enough. For the early crops mild manure such as leaf mould will do well, but leaves not much for the following crop; and if the soil is very poor, a stronger manure will be needed to grow the peas.

Fresh manures and wet mucky soils are to be avoided, as they cause the vines to grow rank and tall: the plants make a great growth in vines, but fail to develop and mature the pods.

Sowings should be begun as soon as the ground is fit to work, and continue at intervals of a week or ten

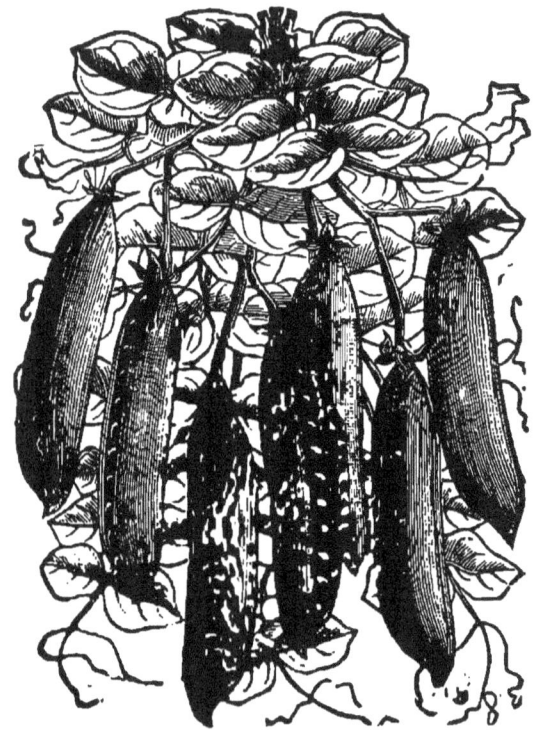

Rawson's Clipper.

days until the first of May. For a continuous supply during the season, make plantings until the last of June; then sowings should be discontinued until the middle of August, when an extra early sort will sometimes produce a grood crop.

All the wrinkled sorts are superior to smooth sorts in every respect except earliness ; they are more delicate in flavor, richer in saccharine matter, and remain longer in season. The market-gardener, however, is not disposed to keep the vines long in bearing, as he usually wants the land cleared for other use. The earliest and the quickest-growing sorts are the best in that case.

Amongst all the numerous varieties offered, the very earliest is undoubtedly Rawson's Clipper. When first brought forward, in the spring of 1886, it had proved on our trial grounds to be the earliest in cultivation. It has now been in the hands of one of our most experienced growers for the past five years, and after careful tests has proved earlier by several days than any other.

It is very uniform in growth and distinct in habit, about thirty inches in height, profusely covered with well-filled pods. It is one of the sweetest and best flavored of the smooth varieties. The entire crop can be gathered in two pickings; it is a very productive and valuable market variety.

Sunol is a variety yet under trial; of great promise as a first early, smooth, round, very productive sort, of superior flavor.

Among the early wrinkled varieties the American Wonder stands at the head of the list. It is very dwarf, averaging eight to ten inches in height, according to the nature of the soil, of the very best quality, and for the home garden at least has no superior for an extra early table pea. Until the introduction of the Wonder, the "Little Gem" was the leading dwarf wrinkled variety, and even now is quite popular. It grows a trifle taller than the Wonder. McLean's Advancer is one of the leading sorts, and a favorite with market gardeners; grows about two feet high, is very productive and nearly as early as Daniel O'Rourke.

The Daniel O'Rourke is a well-known extra early kind, and is quite a favorite with market-gardeners, as the crop may be gathered mainly at one picking. It grows to the height of two and a half feet. The following extra early varieties (as is perhaps generally known) are merely selected stock of the Daniel O'Rourke: First and Best, Maud S., Early Dexter, Carter's First Crop, and many others which are named according to the fancy of the dealer offering them. The Kentish Invicta is almost as early, and a heavy yielder; it is a round blue variety.

Bliss's Abundance is a new early dwarf kind, with large, robust, dark-green foliage; pods from three to three and a half inches long, containing six to eight large wrinkled peas; quality excellent.

Bliss's Everbearing leads all the rest for the general crop. Its pods average four inches long, each containing six to eight wrinkled peas of very extraordinary size, sweetness, and flavor.

Champion of England is the standard late variety. It is a very heavy cropper, and of best quality. Grows about four feet high. The Black-Eyed Marrowfat is the well-known old variety, and grows about the same height and ripens about the same time as the Champion of England. The "Stratagem" is a fine medium-late variety, now well established in favor; excellent in quality, and yields abundantly. It will doubtless long remain a favorite as a market sort, being a heavy yielder, with pods of large size, and having an advantage over other varieties in being easier to pick.

All the late kinds need wider planting than the early dwarf sorts — about four feet between rows is

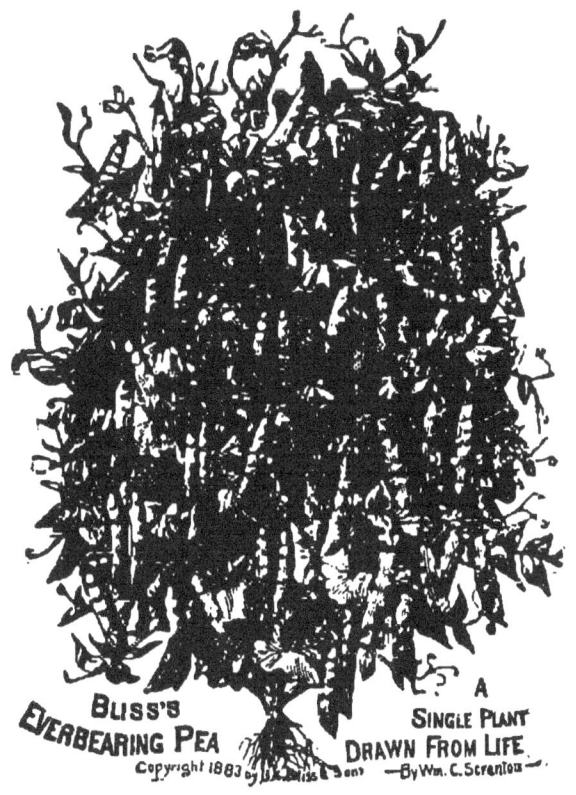

Bliss' Everbearing.

not too much. The number of bushels of pods raised from a bushel of seed peas varies from one hundred to one hundred and fifty; the price (though depressed and irregular as a consequence of shipments from the South disturbing the market, especially as regards the early crop) will average about one dollar per bushel.

PEPPERS (*Capsicum*) are usually sown under glass about April 1st, and should not be transplanted to the open ground until the weather is warm and settled,— say about June 1st, in this locality. They are a family of plants exhibiting very remarkable diversities in shape, size, and color, as well as in the more or less pungent taste by which they are characterized; some changing, as they ripen, from the green color of the young pod to various brilliant shades of red, and others to yellow and orange tints of like intensity — thus becoming in the highest degree ornamental and interesting, but of course not any more valuable to carry to market.

All Peppers require a warm, mellow soil, and heavy manuring applied either before or during growth. The rows may be set eighteen inches apart, and the plants a foot apart in the rows.

Of certain sorts, the pickle factories use large quantities, which are grown at very small prices on contracts; but our market gardeners raise peppers only in very small lots; merely enough to supply the retail trade. The Squash or Tomato-shaped variety is the kind chiefly grown for the pickle factories, and is well adapted, being thick-fleshed, of pungent flavor, very productive, and of good size.

The Bell, or Bull-Nose is a large and mild-flavored variety, and is one of the most popular. The Sweet Mountain, or Mammoth, resembles the Bell in some respects, and is perhaps just as desirable, being similar in shape, not unlike in flavor, and larger; while in the same class with these old and well-known varieties comes the new Ruby King, of larger growth and milder flavor than either — in many respects a superior kind, and unequalled by any other. It commonly attains a size of four and a half to six inches long, by about four inches through. The fruit is so mild and pleasant to the taste that it may be sliced and eaten with pepper and vinegar as is done with tomatoes or cucumbers, and when thus used

Ruby King Pepper.

makes a very agreeable salad. The plant is of a sturdy, bushy habit of growth.

Long Cayenne is the strong pungent variety with which every one is acquainted. It is quite late, and the pods while still young and green are frequently used for pickling. Another very hot and pungent variety, of similar quality but not quite so acrid, and of entirely different habit of growth, is the Red Cluster; in which the small, thin peppers, of a coral red color, stand crowded together in bunches at the top of each branch. It closely resembles the Chili, from which variety it originated.

Still other valuable sorts are: Cardinal (which

Cardinal Pepper.

somewhat resembles Long Cayenne), Monstrous or Grossum, and Child's Celestial.

THE POTATO (*Solanum tuberosum*) prefers soils of a sandy or gravelly nature, although it will succeed, to some extent, on all soils ranging between a light loam and a stiff clay, provided there is just the right amount of moisture. But it is worse than folly to attempt to grow potatoes on land that is waterlogged, or not well and thoroughly drained, either by natural or artificial means. A newly turned sod, other things being favorable, forms the best potato land. In our own experience (especially on land that has been heavily manured for previous crops), the use of stable manure, or of wood ashes, somewhat promotes the "scab;" commercial fertilizers have given us much the smoothest crop. Whatever manuring is applied should, as a rule, be put on broadcast. On some lands, exceptionally light and dry, level culture may prove the best; but we have succeeded better by a moderate hilling up. This seems to keep the land light and friable. Make the cultivator and shovel-plough do all the hilling, and most of the hoeing. For this purpose, put the rows three feet apart. Drop the seed ten or twelve inches apart in the row ; cut to one eye, around which leave a good portion of the substance of the tuber, so that the young growths may have plenty of nourishment until the roots get well established.

Two or three times, before the crop comes up, a smoothing harrow should be run over the piece, destroying the young weeds as soon as they start. The Colorado beetles, or potato-bugs, formerly so much dreaded, are now disposed of very easily by the use of slug shot or Paris green; either is death to the bugs.

The selection and cutting of seed are important points. We recommend medium sized tubers, cut to one eye. The tuber itself is not a seed, but merely an enlargement of the underground stem, and in planting-

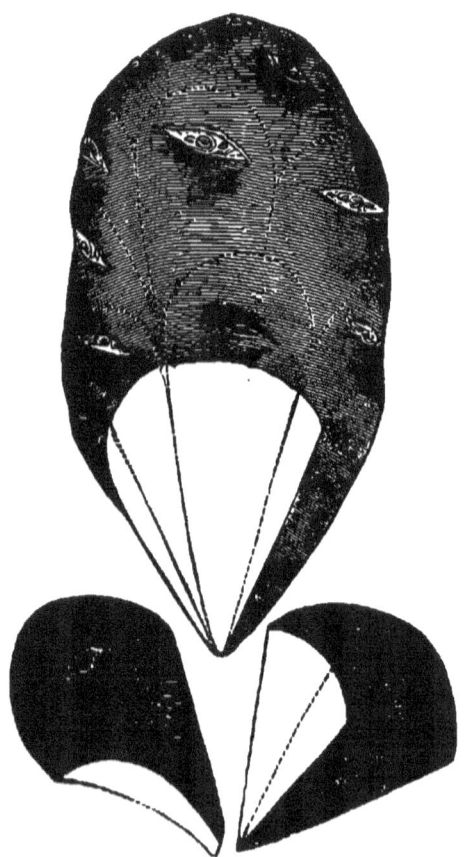

Cutting to One Eye.

ing tubers, either entire or cut, we are putting in (not seeds but) slips or cuttings, in which size is not essential; but probably it is better, as a rule, to use good-shaped, medium sized ones, cut to a single eye.

In a potato tuber held stem end down, it may be seen that the eyes are arranged in regular ascending rotation. For advantageously dividing it to single eyes (as is more especially necessary to those who buy new and valuable varieties), an excellent method is delineated in the cut here introduced. An indentation will be found in each tuber, clearly indicating the stem end. The cuts, to be made with a thin-bladed knife, are all sloped towards it; each cut removes one eye, proceeding, in succession, from the lowest to the highest. Humphrey's Potato Knife is one specially devised, with a blade of curved and concave shape, for cutting out single eyes in general accordance with the above method, and possesses some advantages over an ordinary knife, for that service.

Cultivation of the young plants should commence as soon as they are fairly above the surface of the ground, and continue until the appearance of the blossoms, when no further attention will be required until the time of harvesting the crop.

At each successive hoeing, bring up earth against the plants, adding a little each time both for support to the stalks and also to develop the side-shoots.

For digging the crop, there is at present no more satisfactory implement provided than the digging-fork or the potato-hook. There are, to be sure, already several different implements designed and constructed, and to some extent, perhaps, put to use for employing the labor of horses in loosening and lifting the tubers from the soil. But the best of them — the very latest as well as the earlier ones — have attained but a very moderate degree of success, even when working under fairly favorable conditions ; and in stony or mucky soils will not do the work. There is still a fortune in waiting for the man who invents a completely successful machine-digger.

Varieties are so numerous, and many are so little distinct, that to mention even a quarter of them would be confusing. The Early Rose has an almost endless number of closely related kinds, such as Early Sunrise, Early Gem, Chicago Market, Early Vermont, and others. Standard favorites are the early and late varieties of Beauty of Hebron ; also Clark's No. 1, and Pearl of Savoy. Polaris, a Vermont Seedling, has resisted the rot notably well, is highly productive and of excellent quality. Puritan is a very superior potato, remarkably productive, with white skin and flesh, an excellent and attractive sort. The Snow-Flake is of the highest table quality, but not a great yielder, except in the best land.

Whatever variety is most popular should be chosen to plant for market; and where there is close similarity it is evident that soil and cultivation are of far more importance than choice of a kind.

RADISH (*Raphanus sativus*). Until within the past few years, culture of radishes had been confined to the open ground; but now the growing of this crop under glass has assumed quite important proportions.

For growing in hot-houses the French Breakfast is almost the sole variety used, as it has a short top, is a quick grower, and of good quality. The seed is sown at any time during the cold season, from October to

April. The crop is usually ready for pulling about eight weeks from the sowing of the seed. The temperature should be kept rather low, say from 45° to 60°. Grown in this manner it will be seen that three crops may be grown under the same glass each season.

French Breakfast.

The soil required to grow them to perfection is a loose, sandy loam; and it should be well worked, with a liberal quantity of well rotted manure thoroughly mixed in. The seed is sown in rows about four inches apart; and the plants are thinned to about two inches apart in the row. When about three-fourths of an inch in diameter, they are pulled and bunched, ten in a bunch. The price varies from fifty cents to one dollar per dozen bunches; but, even at the smaller price they are considered a profitable crop.

Scarlet Turnip Radish.

When grown in hot-beds, the Short Top Long Scarlet is preferable to any other. It is usually grown following a crop of lettuce; as, when the lettuce has been grown the heat is then nearly spent, and the loam is in just about the right condition for growing a crop of radishes. It is more suitable than a fresh bed ; which would be likely to stimulate an excessive growth of the tops.

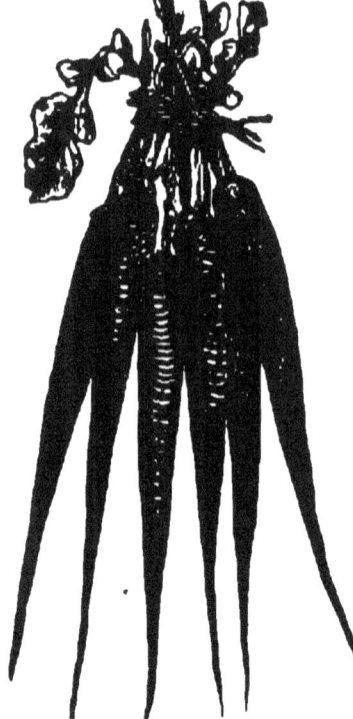
Long Scarlet Radish.

They are grown in rows four inches apart, and thinned to three inches in the row; as this variety (being, when pulled, about the size of clothes-pins) will not so well bear crowding as the French Breakfast. Sometimes a crop of carrots is grown with them ; and, when this is done, every third row is left out for the carrots. After the radishes are taken off, the carrots will occupy the ground to advantage. The glass can be taken from the bed early in the spring and used for some other crop.

In some sections the turnip variety is grown, similar methods of culture being employed; but, for the Boston market, those previously mentioned are raised almost exclusively.

For out-door culture the long-rooted variety is the one chiefly selected. This also succeeds best on a sandy loam, worked very fine and light. It is usually grown in connection with some other crop. The land being made up into beds about six feet wide, each ridge or bed is sown with about ten rows of radishes and four rows of beets, parsnips, or carrots.

In order to have a succession for constant pulling, it is necessary to make sowings every week or ten days, from the first of April to the middle of June. The radishes will require thinning, say to four or more inches apart. When pulled, they are put ten in a bunch, and usually bring three cents per bunch, or $3.00 per hundred bunches (as usually sold). At this price the proceeds per acre would be about $500.

Scarlet Globe Radish

The other crop is not touched until the radishes are removed, but after that it may be cultivated.

Besides the varieties which we have mentioned, the following are grown to some extent in home gardens and for special consumption, viz.: Scarlet Globe and Early Scarlet Olive-Shaped (both good forcing varieties, good also for out-door culture), and Wood's Early Frame, which is somewhat similar to the Long Scarlet, though shorter, and is an early and quite popular sort.

The winter varieties are but little grown. The Black Spanish and Chinese Rose Winter are the leading ones, and when grown for winter use should be stored in sand, in order to keep them fresh.

RHUBARB (*Rheum hybridum*) is now quite extensively grown, both in field culture and forced under glass. It is generally propagated from plants obtained by dividing the heavy, fleshy root, which grows to a considerable size in plants long established; and these are improved by the removal of a part, — also by occasional transplantings to new grounds.

Rhubarb Stalks.

When raised from seed, the sowing is to be done in April, in drills about one inch in depth.

A deep, very rich retentive soil is desirable for growing such large and tender stalks as the market demands, and for bringing them forward in good season. A few days lost or saved in getting into market often makes a difference of one half in the price.

The first pulling of the out-door crop is usually made the last of April or the first of May, and the plants continue to furnish a supply until about the first of July. It is put up in bundles which vary in weight between fifteen and forty pounds, according to the advance of the season, and is sold entirely by weight, the price varying all the way from one to ten cents per pound, and the average returns amounting to between $300 and $400 per acre.

The crop is forced either by setting thickly in hot-beds or hot-houses, or by leaving roots about three feet apart in the ground where they have grown, and setting cold-frames over them. The glass is put on about the first of February. The price on the forced crop varies even more than that of out-door growth; but $5 is a fair estimate of average returns from each 3 x 6 sash.

The two varieties best known here are the Linnæus, early, large, and tender; and the Victoria, also large, but later; of the two the former is the better kind, though both are good.

A newer sort, very superior to either, and in fact better than any other variety known, is the Paragon, earliest of all, and very productive. It is not inclined, as are some other sorts, to run to seed. The leaf is small, while the stalks are large and heavy.

SALSIFY (*Tragopodon porrifolius*). Culture of this vegetable, although limited, is increasing. It is also known under the name of Oyster Plant, or Vegetable Oyster. It should be sown early, in drills fifteen inches apart; the seeds to be covered an inch and a half deep. The crop will succeed best when grown on a light, sandy loam, well enriched and very thoroughly worked before sowing. The after culture is much the same as for carrots or parsnips. The spring supply may, if desired, be left in the ground over winter, as the roots are not injured at all by freezing. In marketing, the roots are tied in bunches of twelve each, none but good-shaped ones being used. Until quite recently there had been but one variety in cultivation, the Long White; although there appeared much room for improvement in size and smoothness of root. We have now the Mammoth, an excellent kind, very smooth and white, growing double the size of the Long White, and of excellent quality.

SEA KALE (*Crambe maritime*). This vegetable produces blanched shoots which are cooked and eaten in

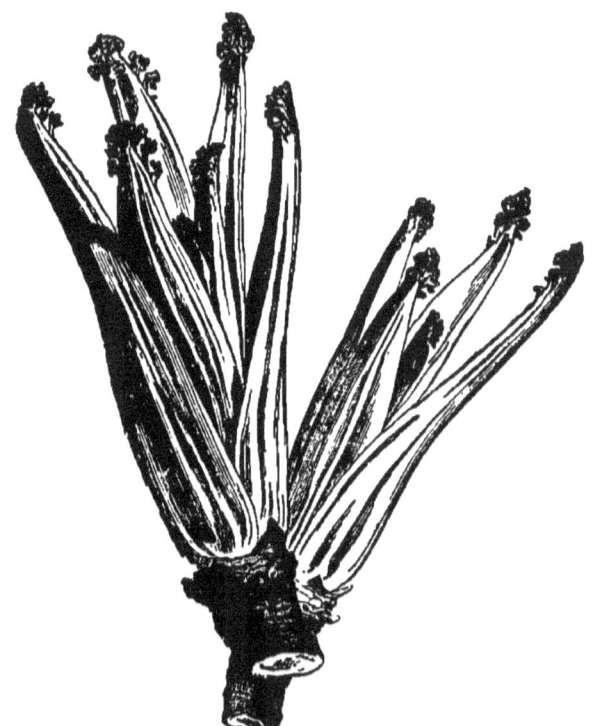

Sea Kale.

the same manner as Asparagus. It is less extensively cultivated than it deserves to be. The seed is sown early in the spring, in drills fourteen inches apart, and covered one inch deep. After the young plants are up, thin to six inches. It is a perennial plant, and requires to be transplanted the following spring, into ground that has been thoroughly trenched and well manured, being then placed in hills three feet apart each way.

Late in the fall, when the leaves have separated from the crown, heap over each plant a shovelful of clean sand, and earth up a ridge a foot and a half high over the rows, from a trenching dug along the space between them, and beat it smooth with the back of the spade.

In the spring, after the cutting is over, the earth should be levelled back into the trenches, so as to expose the crowns of the plants; and a good coat of strong manure should be spread and dug in around them. There is only one variety in cultivation.

SPINACH (*Spinacea oleracea*) is fast becoming one of the leading crops of our market gardens, being sold and used during the whole of the year. For winter use it is usually brought from the South. The crop that comes early in the spring is usually sown about the first of September, and at the beginning of winter is protected with a covering of hay or boughs. This crop generally lasts until about June 1st, when that sown in the spring will be ready for marketing.

It is sold by the bushel. The receipts of an acre when the yield was generally large would be about $200, while if the crop was scarce it might reach as high as $1,000. In spring culture frequent sowings are usually made to furnish a continuous supply.

It is sown in drills, three feet apart, and thinned to about twelve inches apart in the row; though the New Zealand (a very large variety, not much cultivated) requires intervals of two feet or more.

The crop will bear a liberal amount of manure, and for the fall-sown crop a dressing of about seven hundred pounds of sulphate of ammonia is usually given in the spring.

For the spring sowing the Round Thick-leaved is used, and for later use the Long Standing; so-called because it stands longer (by about three weeks) with-

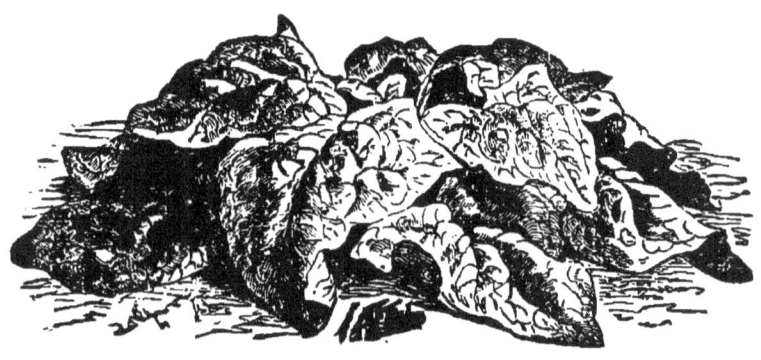

Arlington Pointed Leaf.

out going to seed than any other variety. In fall sowing for spring cutting the Arlington is the favorite as it is choice and hardy. The Prickly, or Fall Spinach, is a prickly-seeded sort, with triangular oblong, or arrow-shaped, leaves, the hardiest of all; mostly used for fall sowings. The Savoy-Leaved is a curled sort of good quality, and very ornamental in appearance.

SQUASHES — PROPER CULTURE. 187

SQUASH (*Cucurbita melo-pepo*) is very largely cultivated for all markets. As it is a tropical plant, in Northern latitudes the season is too short for maturing the later varieties. They are exceedingly tender, and must not be planted in the spring till all danger from frost is over.

There are two quite distinct kinds — Early Bush and Running; the last-named being later. The Summer Crookneck and the Bush Scallop belong to the former. The cultivation of both these varieties is the same. Plant in rows six feet apart, with hills four feet apart in the row.

Bush Scallop.

If the weather at transplanting favors, a week's time may be saved by starting under glass. They mature with us about the 4th of July. In some localities the Bush Scallop is preferred, but in the Boston market the Crookneck is more sought for.

The Early Marrow is planted about the same time, and matures about four weeks later. The hills are put nine feet apart each way; with a liberal amount of seed in each hill, as the plants are just coming on in the height of the bug season. Cover the seed about one inch deep. Manure with about six cords of stable manure per acre, mainly spread on broadcast, but put one shovelful in each hill, and with the latter mix one shovelful of coal ashes to protect them from the borers. When planted with spring greens on ground

Early Summer Crookneck.

Essex Hybrid.

manured with twenty cords per acre, the dressing in the hill may be omitted. The dark, oblong-shaped Marrow is a very salable sort, on account of the color; but its keeping qualities are very poor. The true Boston Marrow is light-colored and quite round, and when planted late will keep almost as well as the Hubbard.

Next in order comes the Bay State; — after it the Turban, which is followed by the Essex Hybrid. The two last named are nearly alike in appearance, the only difference being that the Hybrid has a hard shell. The Hybrid is much the better keeper of the two — is more productive and is also of better quality.

The Bay State is superior to either, uniting in itself a long list of desirable qualities — such as extraordinary weight and solidity of flesh, fineness and dryness of grain, and sweetness of flavor. It has also an extremely hard shell, — always a sign of superior keeping qualities. The color of the shell is green, but the flesh is of a bright golden-yellow. It is equally productive with the Hybrid.

In form and general appearance, it bears some resemblance to the Essex Hybrid, but has a more deeply corrugated surface.

As these later varieties make more vine than the Marrows, they should be planted as much as eleven feet apart each way. They are often put in with a crop of beans or peas, two rows of peas or beans being cultivated in each interval between the squash rows; and these can be harvested and out of the way before the vines crowd upon them. These two varieties reach maturity about the last of August, and continue bearing through September and October, or until frost. The Turban must be marketed soon after picking; but the Hybrid and Bay State may be kept well into the winter.

Among the varieties maturing latest are the Hubbard, Buttman, and Marblehead; of which the first is almost universally preferred. Pike's Peak, or Sibley, belongs to the same class as regards date of ripening, but is thoroughly distinct and is thought by many to be on the whole superior. It is certainly a most excellent sort. It differs in form from all others, in having the stem at the large end; hence may be recognized at a glance. In weight it ranges between eight and eleven pounds. The vine is remarkably vigorous; and ripens its fruit so evenly, that the whole crop may be gathered at one picking; but to obtain the product in its highest perfection it is requisite to house it for some time after the gathering. It will keep, in a good dry cellar, perfectly sound until the last of March, improving meanwhile in quality.

Squashes are sold by weight, with exception of the summer varieties. These are sold by the dozen. The price obtained is very variable. None of the varieties are accounted a paying crop unless they bring at least fifteen dollars per ton.

When picking for storing great care should be taken not to bruise them or break off the stems. They are brought from the fields in wagons and put in piles, to remain until quite dry, and then stored in an even temperature as near 50° as possible.

The Tomato (*Solanum lycopersicum*) holds a high place amongst vegetables in general estimation, both for its use in a fresh state, and for canning and manufacture into catsup; so that its extended and still increasing cultivation is a subject peculiarly important to the market-gardeners of the country. Within the past twenty years, the tomato, from an almost unknown and little considered product of a few small gardens, has grown into popular favor to such an extent that the area of its cultivation is now reckoned in thousands of acres, and will doubtless continue to be further enlarged as population increases; especially about its chief centres, and near the canning establishments.

During this period of expanding cultivation there has been great improvement in varieties, not so much in respect of earliness, perhaps, as in size and quality.

In growing large amounts for particular markets it is not advisable to multiply varieties of the product.

In order to induce a stocky growth, the young plants are twice transplanted. The second transplanting should be made before the plants commence to crowd and grow spindling, and this time they should be put eight inches apart. This last transplanting is always made in hot-beds, but the first is usually made in the house; the plants being put four inches apart.

About the 25th of May the plants sown the middle of February may generally be set in the open ground; and should be planted in rows six feet apart, with plants five feet in the row. The tomatoes usually follow a crop of spinach; and but little additional manure is

will show how it is done:— drive three stakes and fasten barrel-hoops to these. Another very good way is to use only two stakes and a single hoop; these stakes to stand three and half feet high from the ground; and the hoop, which should be broad, flat, and strong, to be well nailed to the stakes at about three feet from the ground.

Hoop Trained Tomato.

With the same object in view, a portable tomato trellis is now made and sold which serves well. Its

PROPAGATION — FORCING — BEST KINDS. 195

construction is simple, cheap, and durable. It is certainly a great convenience in tomato-growing. Either of the foregoing methods serves to prevent the tomatoes from lying on the ground; and thus develops and matures fruit that would otherwise go to decay, or at least fail to ripen off; and, furthermore, greatly facilitates cultivating and gathering the crop.

In this locality the first picking is often made by the middle of July, and at that early date usually brings a good price, sometimes as high as ten dollars per bushel; but the market soon declines, and often falls below paying prices. The average product of an acre may be reckoned at about $400.

The tomato is grown also in hot-houses,— being started in the fall from seed; or may be grown from slips or cuttings. While this method of propagation by cuttings has been recommended and practised by some, especially for the later crop, I think it is far better to grow both late and early crops from the seed; as vines from cuttings are found to be far less productive; and the plants from seed can be secured for any date in the season by timely sowing. For the house-grown product the price is sometimes as high as a dollar a pound; and they continue to yield good profits to the grower until shipments begin to arrive from the South. There are but a very few varieties suited for forcing, and among these the Early Essex is an established favorite. Lorillard and Horsford's Prelude are new varieties especially recommended for forcing.

For out-door culture the varieties catalogued are

numerous enough, but there are few of real merit. Rawson's Puritan has been grown by us for several years as a leading early variety, and has proved not

Rawson's Puritan.

only to be one of the earliest but one of the most profitable in culture as a market variety.

Another early variety is Ignotum, one which well maintains its claim to a front rank among tomatoes; being handsome in color, ripening perfectly throughout, and not inclined to crack or rot.

Atlantic Prize is the first early market variety; of good size and quality; but, of course, the very early sorts cannot be expected to be as solid, nor as good in flavor, as those maturing later.

Only leading varieties have been mentioned.

TURNIPS (*Brassica rapa*). This crop is not very extensively grown in the market garden, as the demand is quite limited. The flat varieties are the only ones cultivated for early marketing.

The soil best adapted to the crop is a sandy or gravelly loam, well enriched and thoroughly worked. The seed should be sown as early in the spring as the ground can be worked, in drills about fourteen inches apart. After the plants have reached the proper size, thin to six or eight inches apart in the drill. By the last of June, in ordinary seasons, they will have reached the size of an ordinary " Boston cracker " and are then ready for bunching.

They are tied five in a bunch and marketed in the same manner as early beets. The Early Milan Purple Top and the Early Purple Top Munich, which closely resemble each other in most particulars, are the principal sorts raised for early bunching, and are certainly as good as any.

The proceeds per acre of a good piece of turnips is about the same as of beets, and the cost of raising is about the same, but on the whole they are not as sure a crop as beets, as they are quite liable to become rough, scabby, and wormy, and consequently worthless.

For fall use, the seed may be sown any time from July 1st to August 20th, and they are often sown with grass seed, using about half a pound per acre broadcast with the grass. Grown in this way, their leaves serve as a protection and a help to the grass plants as soon as they commence to start.

The fall crop is marketed by the bushel, either in the

fall or during the winter as wanted, and may be stored either in cellars or pits. For this crop, the purple Top White Globe, the White Top Strap-Leaved and the Red Top Strap-Leaved are quite desirable varieties.

The Ruta Bagas are almost wholly grown as a farm crop, as they are not sufficiently profitable for the market garden. These may be sown any time during July, and are often used to follow after a crop of cabbage or peas. Sow in drills eighteen inches apart, and thin to one foot apart in the row.

There are no better Ruta Bagas than the best strains of White Sweet German, which are almost universally used both for marketing and home use. The White French, or Rock, is a long, oval turnip, very mild and sweet; the flesh is solid and white, like the German.

The London Extra Yellow Swede, and the Shamrock Yellow Swede, and Carter's Imperial, are the leading yellow-fleshed sorts, and are quite similar to each other in appearance.

WATERMELONS (*Cucurbita citrullus*) are but little grown except as a farm crop, and where land is cheap. They can be readily handled and bear shipping well. What is known as "warm land" is to be preferred for this crop. The soil should be of a sandy or gravelly nature, and it is not important that it should be very rich. Plant as soon as the weather becomes settled; ordinarily about the middle of May. Cover about half an inch deep and press the soil down firmly so as to hold the moisture. Two shovelfuls of manure should be put in each hill, or one in the hill with a light dressing on top. The intervals should be eight feet each way. Five seeds are put in each hill, and the plants, after being well started, should be thinned out so as to reduce the number to three. They require the same cultivation as squash or any other field crop.

Black Spanish is an old reliable variety, very hardy and productive, and excellent for cultivation. The popular Mountain Sweet is a very large oval variety, with a striped skin and thin rind. Gypsy or Rattlesnake, a favorite market variety, is oblong in shape; in color, light green, beautifully striped and mottled. Kolb's Gem, or American Champion, a variety of established merit, is also highly esteemed as a market variety; it carries well, and is of extra fine quality. The Iron Clad is a favorite market variety in many localities. It grows very large, and is a good keeper. The variety called Scaly Bark is distinguished by its rough skin. The rind is unusually thin, but very tough, and it bears transportation to a great distance without injury. The well-known Citron melon is raised entirely for preserving, and is wholly valueless otherwise.

YAM, CHINESE (*Dioscorea Batatas*). Although this vegetable has been grown in this country for several years, it has hardly obtained the popularity which it merits. It is really one of the most valuable esculents in cultivation. The vine will grow to a length of from ten to twenty feet, according to soil and location. The leaves are very dark in color, and heart shaped; the flowers are small, white, and grow in clusters. The root is of pale russet color, oblong, regularly rounded, club shaped, largest at the lower end.

The roots, cut in pieces an inch long, or bulblets,

should be planted at eight inches apart. A deep, light soil, moist and well-enriched, is best adapted to the plant. A well-grown root, two years from the bulblet, should measure two feet in length. They may be cooked either by steaming or roasting; and the flesh will be found very white and of most agreeable flavor.

It would be impossible to find a plant of easier culture, as the roots are perfectly hardy, and can be kept growing year after year in the same location if desired. There is no insect that troubles either the vine or tuber, and no vine can exceed it in vigor of growth. They increase naturally from the small tubers, or bulblets, which form along the vine just above the leaf joints. These should be gathered in the fall, and protected against freezing during the winter. They may be planted any time during the spring, after danger of severe freezing is past. The flowers have a peculiar cinnamon-like fragrance; hence the name "Cinnamon Vine," under which some dealers have sent it out.

When grown in the garden, and merely for the tubers, the vines may be allowed to run on the ground; but if bulblets are desired, these will be produced in greater abundance when poles or other supports are employed to keep the vines up from the soil.

I here bring to a close this discussion of special crops, and their appropriate special culture. In regard to the rules here given, and to the general rules for cultivation which occupy the earlier pages as well — I take occasion to remark that a wide field yet remains open for experiment and enterprise. Every grower should be an experimenter (of course we mean on a prudent and moderate scale), and should habitually report his processes and results for comparison with those obtained by others. He should take pains to observe accurately, and report faithfully and in full detail, all such matters. The various agricultural experiment stations established in different States gladly receive reports so prepared.

The director and his assistants proceed to study and compare the matters so reported. With their peculiar facilities and opportunities they digest and condense the combined experiences of many intelligent observers. Including with these the results of their own more scientific inquiries, they are enabled to put forth publications in continuous series, very valuable to the farmer or gardener, and thereby promotive of the general prosperity of the country.

There are many new and inviting openings for the further study of plants and plant-culture; as, for instance, in electro-culture, now just barely beginning to be practically undertaken; in vegetable and insect physiology, in which much has been learned, and much yet remains to be explored; and in the very many obscure conditions affecting health and growth, quality and quantity of product, and the like.

As instances of appliances already in universal use amongst market-gardeners, yet susceptible of indefinite further modifications and improvement, may be mentioned forcing-houses and hot-beds. Both of these, in their many and very various details of construction and operation, obviously need to be studied as separate (and far from simple) subjects of further inquiry and comparison. On the choice between greenhouse and hot-bed growing, in any given case, or between the many different practicable ways of putting up and operating either, may depend many results involving the true or false economy of the plan; and thus the pecuniary success or failure of the grower.

Thus far in the present work I have had in mind, and mainly confined myself to describing, the growing of crops and use of means and processes which I could recommend as successful from a sufficiently extended experience of my own. In the pages that are to follow, I propose to include, amongst descriptions of tools and other requisites, some of the various means and appliances that are growing into favor though not yet fully established; or that are likely to prove adapted to cases and under circumstances slightly different: in either case worthy of notice as alternatives. These, or some of these, may often prove useful as substitutes for those more familiarly known and used by myself; to which I have given preference, for obvious reasons, in the pages preceding.

CHAPTER VII.

IMPLEMENTS, ORDINARY AND SPECIAL. — FURTHER METHODS AND APPLIANCES. — INSECTS AND PREVENTIVES. — FUMIGATION, HOW CONDUCTED. — FUNGI, AND PLANT DISEASES. — PREVENTIVES. — CONCLUSION.

CONTINUED improvement still appears from year to year in agricultural implements; and some of the tools now used in the market garden and on the farm are of quite recent invention : or have become, through various modifications, entirely different in operation and effect from those in use only three or four years ago; although some of the more common ones, such as are required and in use by every farmer and gardener (hoes, rakes, forks, spades, etc.) have but little changed. The leading American manufacturers of small tools have so nearly perfected the style and quality of these, as to leave practically nothing more to be desired. No other nation can compete with us in the production of handsome, handy, and durable articles of this class.

There is a considerable opportunity for choice,

even amongst small tools of almost the same pattern and make. No good shoveler is quite satisfied unless he can have his own shovel to work with — it fits his hand better than any other. Hoes and forks have their peculiar merits and demerits, such as can hardly be accounted for upon a cursory examination, but in long continued use become apparent. All these, however, involve but little outlay, and their possible peculiarities are, therefore, of less importance to be discussed; but, of course, the clumsy ones should be avoided, or discarded as soon as convenient; and better ones should be watched for, and secured as soon as obtainable. All agree in advising use of the best tools. Good tools make cultivation easier, and crops better in amount and quality. There should be a tool-house, which should also have an outfit for making small repairs. Tools after use should be immediately returned to place. They should always be cleaned off before being left; iron and steel parts should be wiped and oiled, or treated with some more thorough dressing, according to their liability to rust, and the length of time they are likely to remain unused.

Tools operated by horse-power form a large and interesting class of implements, in most of which the steady progress of improvement is very conspicuous. Limits of space will confine us to condensed description — often to a mere brief mention — in treating of these. More detailed description is usually to be had on application to the manufacturers or their selling agents, in the form of elaborate pamphlets, freely illustrated; which (if read with discreet allowance for the bias of their authors) may be consulted with profit for additional information.

The KEMP MANURE SPREADER holds the field alone in its class. As already shown (except under unusual circumstances, or perhaps in the cultivation of a very few crops, of which asparagus, melons, and tomatoes are the chief examples) — the application of manure by a SPREADER is seldom practised by the market gardener because the capacity of these machines is limited to about six or seven cords per acre; but where that amount will suffice, and the spreader is put into service, it gives a very satisfactory result.

We will presume that the use of the PLOW in turning under broadcast dressings of manure has been sufficiently dwelt upon in Part I. and in the cultural directions for special crops. After the manure has been supplied and turned under, the next main requisite in preparing for a crop is to pulverize the soil; and since the PLOW is very efficient in this and other services, in fact quite indispensable, it is manifestly one of the most important of agricultural implements.

Amongst the many varying styles, and different manufacturers, competing for preference, it is a natural question to ask which is the best. There is no complete answer that can be given to this inquiry. Nearly all of the leading styles are of practical use, and each has its own peculiar and individual merits. In certain soils and for certain purposes, one kind of a plow will often be found to do the work and answer the purpose in view better than another, while, under different conditions, the latter might be decidedly the more serviceable of the two.

All the different makes now in favor are good, and some are known to be specially adapted to certain kinds of work. For example, a mould board that lifts and turns the slice very gradually will operate easily, and turn the bottom-side uppermost with the least possible disturbance of the earth;— a shorter mould board with a quicker twist will stir and pulverize the soil. No one need have any difficulty in finding one which will serve his purpose when he knows what he wants.

Sulky-plows, and sulkies attached to ordinary plows, are well adapted for use on level land, when a large amount of work is to be done.

The two-horse land-side plow is the one most used. Even in this class, different makers have different styles, and each claims for his own that it is the best; but every cultivator should judge for himself which is the best adapted to his needs, and endeavor to confirm his judgment by actual trial before purchasing. Much use also is made of the swivel plow. The large-sized or two-horse pattern is chiefly designed for breaking up sod land. It would rarely be needed for this use by market gardeners, but is occasionally required for various other services. A small, or one-horse swivel plow, will often be found very convenient, especially when plowing close to fences. Wherever the land needs to be thrown all one way the swivel pattern comes into requisition.

The different patterns of plows which should be provided include one very large and one of medium size (both land side), and also a sub-soiler. Each of these is to be worked with two horses. As already said, where much plowing is to be done, a sulky is very useful. Provide also one (side-hill or) swivel plow for one horse, two single (or one-horse) land-side plows, and a very small one with double mould board, suitable for going between narrow rows — one which will throw up the dirt but very little.

Next, perhaps, in importance to the plow comes the HARROW. Of harrows, there are almost as many styles as of plows. The cheapness and solid construction of the primitive A harrow with spike teeth and of some others of that class (or approaching it) are about all they have to recommend them. Neither spike teeth, spring teeth, coulters pushed or trailed, nor any similar devices whatever, will fully meet all requirements as pulverizers.

Disk or wheel harrows are now commonly employed. One of the earliest of these, the La Dow, was for a time very extensively used, and generally admitted to be the best pulverizer on the market.

Other implements operating much like the La Dow, and using similar circular disks, are the Corbin, Climax, Warrior, and Reynolds. All have sulky seats and sometimes carry scrapers.

In Clark's Cutaway harrow each disk is in one piece at the hub or centre; but is shaped at the circumference into six small blades, being cut away with deep triangular notches, to obvious advantage.

The Morgan "Spading" is the latest and, I think, best of the wheel harrows, for reasons following, viz : — Solid disks in one revolution bear, substantially, a constant scraping contact to the earth of about four feet. Cutaway disks present a very similar contact, of about two feet in a revolution. Both styles are usually weighted down to perform their work. The Morgan blade or spade is narrow, rounded, and sharp, the end having but about two inches cutting surface, or one foot in one revolution of each set.

The Meeker Smoothing Harrow is employed either for leveling the surface of land, that it may be plowed evenly, or, after plowing, to prepare for the seed-drill.

Every practical cultivator knows the style and construction of a good ROLLER. The nature of the service it performs has already been treated of in preceding pages. A larger use than is ordinarily made of this very important implement is to be recommended.

Next in order of usefulness comes the CULTIVATOR. After the land has been plowed, subsoiled, harrowed, rolled, and planted, this serviceable implement is called into requisition. It executes with thoroughness, dispatch, and economy, a large amount of work that used to be laboriously performed with hand-hoes. Many varieties are offered to choose from, and the choice I recommend may not accord with every one's individual opinion, but I consider the Planet, Jr. (see cut p. 210.) on the whole the best I have ever seen; principally because it can be put into so many different shapes, by varying the combination of its parts, and thus so many different kinds of work can be done with it. The illustrated catalogue of the makers very fully describes its construction, with all its most recent improvements and additional features; and explains the many transformations of which it is capable by interchange and substitution among its different parts, each having special adaptations, and showing great fertility of mechanical contrivance.

In its general operation, it is wonderfully efficient and economical; it stirs and pulverizes the ground, destroying weeds, giving aëration, and promoting moisture about the roots of growing plants; it will throw the earth to or from the rows as may be desired; it does pretty much all that can be done with a hand-hoe in cultivating the crop. Many who are using this implement to-day do not hoe their crops at all by hand work. It requires discretion and skill to obtain such effective results from its use, but there is no question that, in the hands of one who thoroughly understands its capabilities, it can be made to do, at a greatly reduced cost, a large amount of hoeing formerly done with the hand-hoes.

Besides being economical on the score of expense, it is also highly advantageous in enabling the far more rapid execution of the work. Crops often suffer for want of a timely stirring of the soil, especially in times of drought; weeds must be cut down as soon as they show themselves; even when neither weeds nor drought threaten the crops it is beneficial to the soil, and thus to the growing plants, that it should be turned or stirred as frequently as may be, to give it life. Labor with an ordinary hand-hoe is manifestly unequal to carrying out work of this description: it costs too much, and goes over too little ground in a day.

The implement shown in our illustration, under the name of Planet, Jr., Horse-Hoe and Cultivator Combined, meets the exigencies we have described in a thoroughly satisfactory manner wherever the width of planting permits the use of a horse. No farmer or market-gardener can afford to dispense with this or some equivalent form of cultivator. It combines in a single machine, the horse-hoe, cultivator, furrower, and

Planet, Jr., Cultivator.

coverer. The side-hoes or plates are reversible, thus giving double wear; and the levers control adjustments that allow more or less hilling, and also regulate the depth, in conformity with the object or purpose for which it is to be used. This adjustability is a most important feature in suiting its use to various soils or crops, or to various stages of growth. That position of the standards or hoes which is shown in the illustration, is the one which casts the earth toward the rows; but whenever the opposite result is aimed at, it can be arranged for by merely changing their positions, putting each on the opposite side, the work of a few moments only. Although the present age is an age of improvements, and predictions are always rash, I have thought and still consider it next to impossible that this implement will be superseded or very much improved upon.

The hand-hoe most used by market-gardeners is one rather wide and thin, say ten inches by four inches for the blade; and on light sandy land, such as they quite generally have in cultivation, one of this description will be found very much to be preferred. The shovels used are of two kinds, one with short handle and square blade, the other with a long handle and round point. The former is always employed for putting the heating material into hot-beds, the square part being convenient for making the bottom of the bed smooth and even. The long one serves best for banking celery and ordinary work around the fences and buildings. The spade is a tool that is little used except to dig horse-radish and roots, and occasionally for digging celery when it is large and cannot be thrown over with the plow.

The six-tined and five-tined forks are the ones most used for pitching manure, digging in hot-beds, and all the work done with a fork; but the spading-fork is also a very useful tool; expressly adapted to loosening and throwing over garden soil. It is made with only four tines; these are either flat or angular in shape, with but little to choose between the two styles.

The SLIDE-HOE is used mostly between the rows of beets, lettuce, spinach, onions, dandelions, parsley, celery, and all the crops sown by machine. This tool is made in different widths so as to fit the varying intervals between the rows for which it is intended. The smallest are four inches wide, and they are made to range upwards to nine inches. They are used by sliding them in a direction parallel with and along the row, and the knives enter the soil to a depth of about one inch, making the land loose and light on the top, and destroying the weeds.

Arlington Slide Hoe.

THE LITTLE GEM WHEEL HOE is a hand implement, combining some of the characteristics of the horse-hoe, or cultivator, and the slide-hoe; thus producing a very serviceable tool. It is well-proportioned, as regards size, to the work to be done; built light and strong; all iron and steel, except handles; well made, and handsomely finished, and adjustable in every way. It is made with single wheel, for use between the rows; and also with double wheel, for use astride the rows.

Wheel-hoes for similar service are likewise made and sold by the Planet, Jr., manufacturers, who continue to maintain their well-known high standard of excellence in all goods of this class. Moreover, the wheel-hoes of their design possess unrivalled advantages of adaptation to different kinds of work, by reason of their many possible transformations. These are very ingenious; for description, see pp. 215-216.

SEED SOWERS.

THE SEED-SOWER OR DRILL is one of the most useful and labor-saving implements in the entire outfit of the market garden. It is used to sow nearly all kinds of seed. Even peas and beans are ordinarily sown by this machine. The quantity of seed sown is regulated by small tins, with holes affording passage for the seeds to the exact amount required, and the distance between rows is regulated or marked by a chain which is made to drag from an adjustable arm. While one row is being sown, the next one is marked by the chain.

Arlington Seed Drill.

The adjustable arm is a stick pierced with little holes, and placed across the handles of the machine. The depth of the sowing is regulated by raising or lowering the tooth which ploughs a little furrow for the seed to drop in. The seed may be sown from one-fourth of an inch to three inches deep, and is covered by two little blocks, so arranged as to draw the dirt over upon the seed. This is followed by a roller, which is regulated by a spring so as to roll heavy or light as may be desirable. The machine represented in the illustration is called the Arlington seed drill. It is altogether the best one ever seen by me, is very generally used by market-gardeners in the vicinity of Boston, and every one who has it in use approves it highly. It has a large wheel, some twenty-eight inches in diameter, with a broad rim, two and one-half inches, which prevents it sinking into the mellow earth, and runs so easily that it can be used all day without fatigue to the operator. It sows fine seeds with perfect regularity, as well as the larger seeds.

The Little Gem drill is small but efficient. It was devised in response to a general desire among small gardeners for an inexpensive drill which will do perfect work; and it satisfies this demand completely.

Still other seed-sowers are, the Matthews', the Monitor, and the Planet, Jr.

For the planting of corn, beans, and other seeds of the larger class, and for use on rough or stony land, the need is met by such machines as the Billing's, Albany, or Eclipse. All these are to be run with a horse; and are supplied with fertilizing attachments for depositing, properly distributed, any requisite amount of dry fertilizing powder at the same time with the seed.

Each year competition in market gardening and root growing makes garden seed drills more necessary. With their assistance, seed sowing can be done with so much greater regularity, rapidity, and ease, and with such large saving of seed as well, that the planting of a very small acreage is sufficient to warrant the purchase of a tool which is now made so reliable, simple, and inexpensive.

THE PLANET, JR., combined drill, wheel-hoe, cultivator, rake, and plow was in its primary form a seed sower; and has been made adaptable to many of the various subsequent operations requisite in vegetable culture by various ingenious cultivating attachments. The change from a seed-drill to a wheel-hoe can be made in a few moments by taking out two bolts, and putting on the hoes.
These can be safely set to cut within an inch of the rows at the first hoeing of small plants from seed. — The cut shows this hoe working among onions at first hoeing; — it is then that careful and close work counts.

Planet, Jr., Wheel-Hoe.

The method here shown is of course applicable, equally, to all crops when small. It is not necessary to watch the course of the blades, but only to keep the row exactly between the wheels. If desired, in place of the hoe-blades, a pair of cultivator-teeth may be used, for mellowing the soil effectually, while causing less lateral disturbance of the surface.

Subsequently, when the plants are of larger size, the cultivation is performed by propelling the hoe between the rows (instead of astride). A single cultivator-tooth being attached, centrally, in addition to the two hoe-blades shown in the cut, the entire space between the rows is covered and worked into mellow condition by one passage of the tool, — every weed being destroyed. The width may be adjusted to suit all rows not wider apart than sixteen inches.

By another obvious modification, replacing the two hoe-blades, used in the last described combination, by cultivator-teeth, we obtain a *three-tooth cultivator*, for stirring and mellowing between the rows without causing any (general) lateral movements of the soil.

The Plow Attechment.

The hoe-blades may be attached so as to throw either toward or from the rows. By other and similar changes, it may be readily turned into a ten-toothed rake, useful for light cultivation, or, again it becomes a handy little plow, for light furrowing and covering. Other details may be gathered from the illustrated pamphlet issued by the manufacturers.

I consider the *improved pattern* of 1891, styled the " P. Jr. Double Wheel Hoe, etc." to be the most desirable. It is built with sole adaptation to the cultivation of the rows. A separate implement is put to service for sowing and covering.

TOOLS FOR SPECIAL USES. 217

RAWSON'S FIELD MARKER is a very useful tool. It will work either ten, twelve, twenty or twenty-four inch

Rawson's Field Marker.

intervals by simply changing the pins in the wheel (which are put in with a nut) and will mark as fast as a man can walk. It is found especially useful in setting out cabbage, cauliflower, celery, lettuce, etc. After once using this implement, no farmer will be willing to be without one.

Lettuce Bed Markers.

The two markers intended for lettuce, and shown in the cut, are used in marking the beds for lettuce to be grown under glass. One marks five rows — one under each row, or light, of glass, when there are five lights wide in each sash, of six inches each. The other is then used to mark ten places for plants in each row, thus making fifty plants under each sash. The bed is prepared with the sash off, and when the sash is to be put in place over the bed each space is marked, by the two men putting on the glass; the one on the lower, or front side, using the one with the handle, and the man on the back side using the other marker.

A rake-handled marker with ten teeth, is also made for sowing radishes or cabbage or lettuce. Mark the rows by drawing the teeth from the back side of the bed towards the front, bearing down so as to make the furrows deep, if required; and always making the first tooth of the marker follow for a guide the row just made by the last tooth, thus making nine rows under each sash four inches apart.

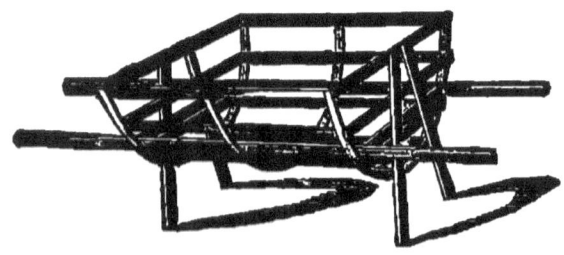

Cabbage Carrier.

The Cabbage Carrier is very useful. It is light and durable, and can easily be carried between the rows of cabbages. It is made of such size as to hold all that two men will want to carry.

GREENHOUSE HEATING. — We have supplied on a preceding page figures for making ready estimates of the piping needed. These figures are based upon our own experience in structures of ordinary proportions. For instance, the general cross-section of one of the author's greenhouses in Arlington has dimensions frequent in ordinary practice, viz : Height at the back 10 feet; height at front 4 feet; under the ridge, that is, at the highest point of the interior, 15 feet; span, 33 feet. The length of this structure is nearly 400 feet. [See inset facing page 72.]

These figures, of course, indicate a definite interior cubic content; and from the heating by pipes actually done there I have derived rules which admit of ready application, for all buildings substantially similar; even though somewhat differing in height of front or rear wall, pitch of roof, etc., and of any less or greater length, likely to be erected for the purposes of the vegetable grower. [See pp. 72, 73.]

A more elaborate calculation may generally be had, (free of charge to the party contemplating the outlay) together with estimates for doing the work, from any of the numerous establishments that stand ready to contract for and supply modern heating equipment in its various forms. In such calculations it has been common to reckon from the glass surface actually present in the given case. A method still more precise consists in reckoning from the whole exposed surface of the structure; glass, sides, and ends; rating the two latter as of one-third the radiating effect resulting from a similar surface of glass.

A convenient hand book has lately been issued by the Herendeen Mfg. Co., of Geneva, N. Y., devoted to the subject of heating by hot water or steam, with reviews and descriptions of the different methods employed for piping greenhouses on either system. It comprises much valuable information clearly conveyed, and tables handy for computation. Hot water has lately been piped in a new way, — by the use of much smaller pipes than formerly; and any one interested will do well to procure the book, in which this new method is favorably mentioned and fully described.

ELECTRO-CULTURE. — In my Arlington greenhouse, above mentioned, is afforded an example of successful and profitable use of the electric light in stimulating plant-growths. Four 10-ampere, 45 volt, Brush arc lamps of 2,000 nominal candle-power are employed, when the beds are occupied with lettuce, with the effect of causing the growth of this crop to be maintained continuously instead of being intermitted at night; this saves time, if not quite proportionately, at least in a material degree; accelerating the maturity of the crop, and enabling the cucumber plants, which are to follow, to begin their growth so much the earlier.

On the inset plate, in fig. 1, the appearance of plants in the ordinary or dark greenhouse is exhibited; and in that which is subjoined may be noted the increased size and more rapid growth of other plants under the electric light, all other conditions being similar.

I have not yet extended my use of the electric light to the culture of other crops than lettuce; and believe there is ground for thinking that some at least

Fig. 1. — Lettuce in Ordinary Growth.

Fig. 2 — Lettuce under Electric Light.

will be injured, rather than benefited, by that treatment. Except in the case of lettuce, other experimenters have found such results as leave it still a problem whether it can be used to advantage. Some experiments made at Ithaca, N. Y., indicate that it is better to intermit the use of the electric lamps during some portion of each night, and always on moonlight nights. The employment of the ordinary white opal globes, — to temper or modify the bare unshaded light (when run continuously),— also appeared, in those experiments, to be beneficial, but I have net used them.

For the forcing of asparagus and other perennials, Permanent Outside Beds are sometimes used. These beds are so constructed as to afford a substitute for the more convenient but highly expensive equipment of hot-houses having water or steam pipes for supply and regulation of heat. As they involve a much smaller initial outlay, they may be considered as affording, under certain circumstances, a more desirable method.

Where such a bed is proposed, the plan generally followed is to surround the bed by a trench bricked up on the outside and filled with stable manure. As often as may be required by the temperature, the manure is renewed. The bed may be four or five feet wide, and as long as desired; of course, covered with glass. If made six feet wide, the ordinary 3 x 6 glass can be used, which is more convenient; and, in such case, it is desirable to have box flues leading across through the centre of the bed from one trench to the other in order to promote distribution of the heat. Sometimes there is only one trench, running lengthwise through the centre of the bed, thus dividing it into two narrow ones.

The growth made in forcing-houses enclosing temporary beds is thought, however, to be rather more profitable in the final result. It is usual to make the temporary bed three feet wide; and for asparagus the rows are put one foot apart, with the plants eighteen inches apart in the row. Such close planting will need heavy manuring and close attention.

If a cheap house for forcing asparagus, etc. in early spring is as much as is aimed at, the following plan, recommended in "The American Garden," is as good as any. It may be made either as a double or single span; if double span, 8 or 10 feet wide. Build a wall from the frost line to a foot above ground. Frame and cover with glass. If the drainage is not good, it must be made so. Dig a trench two feet wide through the centre for a walk. Make an excavation several feet square at one end, to serve for the furnace or stove, and also for the entrance. To heat the beds, carry the smoke around the outside of the bed in flues which are almost entirely below the surface of the ground, the smoke finally passing out of the chimney. Near (and for some distance from) the furnace, build the flue of brick to prevent fire, but the rest construct of boards. In summer the sash can be removed, and in winter it would be better to apply a mulch and cover the frame with boards rather than the sash, as it would be more apt to give an equal temperature.

Arrange the beds on each side of the walk, and plant as has been above described for temporary beds in forcing-houses. It will be remembered that where so little earth is allowed to each plant it is necessary to manure often and heavily.

PUMPING OUTFIT. — We have already (Part I.), given a general outline of apparatus for water supply and distribution; and will here repeat the remark that, there being a wide field for choice in selecting and arranging the various requisite features, and the outlay usually being large, prudence demands a careful study in advance of all attendant conditions and circumstances. Then, after one has made for himself the best scheme he can individually devise, and before embarking his means in the execution of it, it will pay to call in the services of an expert, skilful enough to comprehend the particular case, and to utilize in it the experience of a large professional practice. It will not do, however, to leave all to him; the proprietor must make it his own business, none the less, to understand the whys and wherefores, and to take no step of which he cannot feel he clearly understands the method and the reason.

Amongst the first questions to be weighed and decided is that concerning steam boilers and windmills — which, or whether both (or whether either), — shall be utilized for power. The pump must be one adapted to the power employed. In case wind and steam are both put to service, two separate and distinct pumps will usually be required. With steam, the direct-action horizontal pumps, (of which the

Deane pattern, shown in the cut, is a good example), are well adapted for the work. Various makers of steam pumps offer various other patterns which are good and efficient, or may be presumed to be so, from the fact that they divide the market demand, with no distinct essential superiority evident in either.

Minor circumstances commonly determine one's

Deane Boiler and Pump.

choice. If any one pattern were positively and essentially superior, it would not take long for the others to drop out of sight, — so thoroughly have been the respective merits and demerits of all such apparatus established by long continued tests, in widely extended service. Simplicity of action is important, but this condition does not (at least in all cases) exclude belted or geared connections. The best arranged windmill pumps are "geared back" — though probably the majority of those at present in use work the pump-rod by direct attachment to the crank-pin.

Our own experience, already given, as regards the power to be employed has extended only to wind and steam. But there is yet another means for filling the irrigating tanks or mains. It consists in employing the power of one or more horses, working in a horse power machine, suitably constructed and solidly geared in combination with a powerful suction and force pump; drafting the water from the well or supply main, and raising it to the storage tank.

Horse Power Draft and Force Pump.

This constitutes a complete and self-contained pumping outfit. It has the same advantage over windmill pumping that steam power possesses, in being always reliably at hand. It requires no skilled labor for its operation; a feature which commends it as especially suitable for small cultivators.

The illustration here given will obviate the necessity of a further description of its construction. Its capacity of delivery is 4,500 gallons per hour, (seventy-five per minute) at 50 revolutions. The work required of the team varies, of course, with the height of lift; and may be readily computed for any given case. The machine is supplied with three one-horse draft-bars, but one horse will easily work the machine at the given rate, in pumping against a head of thirty feet, and even more than that. This combination of pump and horse power is quite a novelty — at least in its present form; we cannot very definitely say how far, or how often, it can be advantageously used.

As above said, we may be reasonably confident that a pump of any leading style, purchased from a reputable dealer (including, too, its steam cylinders and fittings, if a steam pump), will be found pretty nearly what it is represented. But in choice of boilers, and wind-mills likewise, neither general experience, nor opinions gathered from dealers, will be found, perhaps, quite so safely reliable.

Of one point, already dwelt upon, the vegetable grower may be wholly confident: that, in some way or other, as an indispensable necessity, he must procure water. In making his choice of means for doing it, he will do well to weigh carefully what we have here suggested, as regards alternatives; but on the main matter, there is no alternative — the water must be had, as an indispensable provision, to save his entire scheme of cultivation from absolute failure; to make it even *possible* to raise crops that will pay.

INSECTS, AND PREVENTIVES. — So extensive and serious is the destructive work of injurious insects that — except on such land as is kept under continual tilth and subjected to constant and thorough cultivation, with judicious rotation of crops — it often seems if as the bugs must get the upper hand of the grower, do what he may. Bugs of one kind or another are found eating everything that grows in the shape of useful vegetables; but never attack a weed.

Unlike the mildews and other fungous parasites, insects are nowise discouraged and driven off by healthy and vigorous growth in the plants — this is just what they like to find. Sometimes they will sweep off every plant in an early stage of growth; or they may delay their coming till just before harvest and then consume the entire crop.

The Wavy-striped Flea-beetle (*Haltica Striolata*) is very destructive to young cabbages and turnips. As soon as the young cabbages appear above the ground it attacks them by eating off the seed leaves; later, when the second leaves appear, the danger lies in another quarter, and it will often be noticed that the plant wilts and changes color. The grub has eaten away the roots.

Professor Hulst recommends, for suppression of this insect, the kerosene emulsion, one part of the oil to twelve or fifteen parts water. In planting out cabbages the roots should be dipped in the emulsion; and thereafter, at intervals of about two weeks, enough of this compound should be poured around the base of the stalks to saturate the earth to the depth of at least an inch, whether the maggots appear to be present or not.

The same insects that attack young cabbage plants, and the turnips, also infest the radish. In some localities it is almost impossible to grow radishes of a size fit for the table before they are practically destroyed by a small maggot. This maggot appears to be the larva of a fly, closely related to those so destructive to the onion. If radishes, cabbages, cauliflowers, and onions are growing in adjacent rows it has been found that the fly will attack all the rows successively; taking the radishes as first choice and proceeding to the rest, usually in the order named.

The onion fly lays her eggs on the leaves of the young and small onion plants, near the ground. They soon hatch, and the maggots at once attack the bulb. In about two weeks after this a second brood of flies appears, to be followed by more maggots. The remedy at this stage consists in removing every infested bulb. These may be known by the leaves turning yellow. They cannot be pulled up by the tops without risk of letting the maggot escape from the decayed bulb. They must be lifted by a trowel, or an old knife, so as to be sure to bring up the maggot. The bulbs so removed, and the maggots, must be burned. Strong caustic lime-water, and concentrated solutions of kainit or muriate of potash are said to be safe and sure remedies when applied in time. A pint, or half-pint of the liquid is to be poured upon every plant, making sure of reaching the infected root. This will kill the eggs in the ground as well as the maggot in the root — by simple contact. Plants once seriously affected can hardly ever be saved.

The squash and pumpkin, the cucumber, and the melon all belong to the *Cucurbitaceæ*, or Gourd family. Hence, naturally, the same insects infest all these related plants. The squash bug is one of the worst and most disagreeable. When handled or disturbed, it gives off a very repulsive odor. The insects are quiet during the day, but at night lay their eggs in little patches, of a brownish yellow color, and glued to the leaves. They are quite easily kept under control by handpicking. The same means is practised with the tomato-worm and the potato-bug. In the case of the latter, however, the free application of Paris green to the vines is less laborious and equally effective.

Wire-worms are frequently found infesting the soil prepared for the greenhouse; but can be suppressed by the addition of three or four pounds of unslacked lime to the bushel of soil. Similar treatment may be presumed to be beneficial when they appear in outdoor culture.

The white grub is a serious source of trouble to cultivators, and no application has yet been found by our gardeners to afford a satisfactory means of destroying them. It seems that if left lying in the ground, in winter quarters, the grub may be frozen to a solid lump, but when thawed out in the spring will be full of life and vigor. Late fall plowing, as already recommended on a preceding page, serves to bring it to the surface, exposing it more effectually to the cold and to its natural enemies, thus to some considerable extent reducing its numbers. But the most hopeful treatment yet proposed is that recently put forward by French entomologists who claim to have discovered a plant-parasite by aid of which lands thoroughly infested with the white grub have been very largely relieved after a two-months' trial, and so as to afford a reasonable prospect for the complete extirpation of the pest. This remedy, of introducing a parasite harmless in itself but destructive of the noxious insect, is similar to that which has been so successfully applied in the case of the scale-insect in the vineyards of California.

Insecticides in liquid solution may be applied by use of suitable force pumps, or garden engines (according to the scale on which the operation is to be carried out), equipped with spraying nozzles.

But there are drawbacks and difficulties in the use of liquid solutions: one is that the poison does not actually dissolve in the water, which has to be constantly agitated to maintain a mixture. Another is the great weight of the quantity required to be used. Dry mixtures are therefore employed, being dusted over the plants. They should be put on preferably when the foliage is still damp after a rain or dew; and may be applied by use of a very fine sifter. Metal canisters, having finely perforated bottoms, are made and sold for this purpose, to be used in the same manner as an ordinary pepper caster. These will answer in a small way only.

A capital implement for applying dry mixtures to field crops is the "Farmer's Favorite" Duster. In operating this device, the left hand is held firm, while the right hand rotates the reservoir of poison and diffuses it effectively.

Any device such as described will, however, be limited to use upon low-growing crops; and, moreover, it will obviously serve to distribute the powder only upon the upper surfaces of the foliage, while many insects, and especially the eggs by which they multiply, may be found snugly harbored on the under side. To meet this deficiency (when the case is one requiring it), use is made of a bellows of peculiar construction, supplied with a convenient receptacle for the powder to be distributed, from which it escapes gradually into the nozzle of the bellows when operated. It is made in various patterns and sizes, all operating in substantially the same way. There are other implements that can be used, but they are of inferior efficiency, and have nothing to recommend them except in being sold at a lower price. The best, in this as in many other things, will be found the cheapest.

Changing the crop affords a partial preventive against the inroads of insects, providing that the change is to an entirely different family of plants; for it is well known that the continued cultivation in one locality of any particular crop has a tendency to assemble there all its peculiar enemies, and favors their rapid multiplication.

No absolutely complete preventives are known; and cultivators must recognize the necessity of constant exertion, and unremitting use of the best known and most efficient of those now in use. Due inquiry and fuller knowledge of facts might help to accomplish much toward limiting, if not wholly exterminating, each and every kind of pestiferous insect. Neighbors should combine, both for observation and action; first to devise, and then unitedly to pursue, such measures as promise substantial relief. For instance, take the case of the pea weevil. If all the farmers of the country should unitedly forbear to raise peas for a single year it would die off completely. Perhaps a means of relief less radical and more practicable of execution may yet be discovered; but none is now known to exist.

FUMIGATION, HOW CONDUCTED. — Fumigation for the suppression of the aphis or green-fly (sometimes called green louse) on lettuce has been already recommended in our cultural directions for growing that plant. We employ moistened tobacco stems in this case. Tobacco in any form is repulsive to the aphis, which is often driven away from lettuce by strewing the stems on the soil about the plants. As a liquid application, a decoction of hot water and tobacco stems diluted to the color of weak tea may be used with good results. For the destruction of the black louse, an insect apt to infest the cucumbers in forcing-houses, the removal of the first affected leaves is generally practised. Tobacco fumigation seems ineffectual in the case of this insect.

The method of fumigation is, of course, not applicable to out-door cultivation; but is extensively employed, and forms an efficient means of prevention and relief, in all hot-houses. Vapor of sulphur is regarded as a good means of controlling powdery mildews.

Fumigators offered in market are made of strong galvanized sheet iron, 20, 24 or 28 inches high, of diameters 13, 14 and 16 inches; the larger size containing one bushel, the others three fourths and one half, respectively. Each is supplied with a firing door and a perforated cover, and with convenient handles for lifting and transporting.

In a house such as shown in photogravure facing p. 72, which is 33 feet span, 15 feet high at the ridge, and nearly 400 feet in length, containing about 130,000 cubic feet of interior space, I employ four of the largest sized ones. These require to be operated only an hour, or perhaps a little more, to fumigate the entire building effectively. Such a fumigation having been repeated three nights in succession is then intermitted till another time arrives when it seems to be needed, or might be prudently employed as a preventive.

Vapor of sulphur may be obtained by use of a kettle or basin containing sulphur (brimstone) heated nearly to the boiling point, and kept at that heat as long as the process is desired to continue. A small kerosene stove and an iron kettle form a convenient and manageable equipment. Vapor enough should be generated to visibly fill the house or apartment, and give off a noticeable odor. But the sulphur must be carefully watched to prevent its taking fire, in which event fumes would arise destructive to all plant life, and might do extensive mischief.

FUNGI, AND PLANT DISEASES. — PREVENTIVES. — Disease in plants manifests itself in various forms, amongst which we recognize two distinct classes; one due to the presence of animal parasites, insects and their larvæ, such as above described; while the other includes smut, mildew, blight, rust, and all similar fungous or vegetable parasite growths, which we group under the general name of Fungi.

It is often not clearly evident to which of these two classes, or whether, indeed, to either of them, the trouble really belongs. Some believe it is an insect which causes the "blight" in celery; but I do not agree with that view. I know an insect does appear on the leaves when they begin to decay; but on almost every different kind of decaying vegetation some one insect peculiar to it is apt to appear, corresponding to *saprophytes* among fungi, — being invited by the decay, but not the occasion of it.

And often, when the insects have made their appearance, and the leaves are already yellow, if there is a sufficient application of water, either by the occurrence of a heavy rain or artificially supplied by irrigation, the insects will disappear, the yellow leaves will drop away, and the plants will grow healthy again, with a good crop as the result. The renewed vitality of the plant enables it to cast off the morbid condition, however originating.

This view points us to the main remedy or preventive of all disease, — and more particularly the chief preventive against every form of vegetable parasite, viz., clean and nourishing culture. In the outset this is the means, and the only means, to be relied upon. This is the first requirement; of course there are others. Hurtful conditions may be noted and avoided. It may reasonably enough be assumed that plants are liable to forms of disease attributable neither to vegetable nor animal parasites, but arising much like disorders in animals, as from imperfect nourishment, excessive cold or heat, lack or superabundance of moisture, and the like unhealthy conditions. Mismanagement of heat, or moisture, on forced crops frequently entails a blight; or promotes mildew, as elsewhere described in treating of the culture of lettuce. A succession of dark days, depriving the plant of sunshine, exerts a similar influence; unless relieved by aid of the electric light, now beginning to be used.

So too, some harmful element may exist in the soil or fertilizer, causing the plants to languish; and thus again the spores of fungi may be enabled to fasten upon them. It is good policy, alike as against the fungous and all other disorders, and on general grounds as well, to put all the vigor we can into the growing plants. We should also bear in mind the great importance of prompt and efficient action wherever disease is apparent; as it will surely and rapidly extend itself, unless controlled.

Owing, perhaps, to the fact that the varieties and habits of insects have been more obvious objects of study, there has been collected, thus far, comparatively little scientific knowledge concerning fungous diseases of plants, and their appropriate remedies; but vegetable growers have, from practical experience, acquired much valuable information (though leaving much yet to be learned) and have been led to devise and apply remedies, some of which are very successful.

Fungi that live upon dead and decaying substances, such as toad-stools, black and blue moulds, and the like, are of little interest to the cultivator; but there is another class, of entirely different habit, that attacks living plants, pushing its own rootlets into the growing leaf or stem or root, and taking its sustenance from the juices so obtained. Plants grown in forcing-houses are especially subject to these attacks. Among these fungi are the downy mildews, like those on spinach and lettuce; and the powdery mildews, such as attack cucumbers.

They multiply through the agency of spores, as plants by seeds. Some of these spores develop with great activity in a summer temperature, natural or artificial, when other conditions are favorable, but are readily destroyed when exposed to severe cold, long continued drought, etc., or to certain artificially created conditions. Others, however (called resting-spores), more sluggish in habit but of more endurance, are found to remain unaffected, preserving the species; so that their complete extinction in any locality is not to be expected, in the present state of our knowledge.

As a rule, when a vegetable parasite fastens upon a plant, it is next to impossible to kill the parasite without destroying the plant by the same operation. It is obvious, therefore, that no treatment can be judicious which is not mainly preventive.

Healthful condition is, as already urged, an important means of prevention. Another, which has been often recommended, but far too little attended to, consists in the removal and destruction of all leaves, twigs and dead growths which may contain the spores.

The various liquid preparations for spraying and so protecting the foliage and succulent stems, by way of which the spores are apt to gain footing on growing plants, generally operate by coating the surfaces with a thin film of some substance in which the spores cannot germinate, while yet it is harmless to the plant. The spraying should be repeated, at intervals of ten or fifteen days at most, at such time and as long as any danger of an attack is to be apprehended. This time varies with the different habits of different fungi ; further knowledge than we now possess on that point will doubtless be gathered as time goes on.

IN CONCLUSION.

I AM very sure that much in the preceding pages will be directly helpful in the way of practical guidance to any one engaged, or about to engage, in the business of vegetable growing. Indirectly, also, the cultivator or student will be benefited, if, by their perusal, he is stimulated to a livelier sense of the variety and importance of the multiplied details belonging to his chosen avocation.

Wherever there has not been opportunity for the full discussion of any subject, in adequate proportion to its prominence and practical importance, I have endeavored to make such suggestions as will lead the thoughtful reader to enquire further, and learn more.

The rules herein laid down are, in compact form, the net results of extended practical experience. They are no haphazard inventions, of doubtful utility, as are too many of the instructions and cultural directions which, from time to time, obtain more or less currency amongst horticulturists.

Learners, in conducting experimental work of their own, or in considering results as reported by others, should beware of hasty conclusions. There are always manifold obscure conditions affecting largely, perhaps controlling, the outcome of crop experiments. Of these conditions, the very ones least recognized and understood may have far more to do with results, than those he has been most intent on observing.

Results of vegetable-culture will always be largely affected by climatic conditions; and these, of course, are variable from season to season. Crops will sometimes fail utterly,— and again sometimes succeed astonishingly, — for no visible reason in either case. Manure effects, especially on soils naturally poor, are apt to be very difficult of prediction, or subsequent analysis: the only safe general maxim being the common-sense rule, to feed the plants abundantly and let them find and take what they require.

The conditions of greenhouse and hot-bed culture are more definitely known, and can be more exactly fulfilled, than those of open culture, for obvious reasons. It is in these forms of vegetable growing that the largest recent advances have been made, and in which the most important future improvements seem likely to be developed.

As regards choice and rare winter-products of forcing-houses, the market demand, though steadily increasing, is but small as yet. Those who have access to the larger markets are, of course, comparatively far better enabled to make suitable disposal of such products. Others will be limited, for the present, to producing the more common kinds, such as lettuce, dandelion, and parsley, for which a more general demand exists. The rarer sorts, such as asparagus, cucumbers, cauliflowers, and tomatoes, being still regarded as special luxuries, can be freely disposed of only in the large cities.

That the cultural directions foregoing and other matter presented leave much to be learned, and are, taken by themselves, only partially adequate to the guidance of the unskilled cultivator, is only what must be true of any similar manual. It would be hard to name a subject open to wider research and capable of greater advances than is that of plant-growing, even when limited to its most practical aspect.

SUCCESS IN MARKET GARDENING demands intelligence, diligence, and natural aptitude. Personal diligence and natural aptitude are matters outside the scope of any manual; but an *intelligent cultivation* of the various crops under all the varying conditions of the business can, of course, be promoted greatly by referring to the experience acquired by those who have succeeded in it.

www.ingramcontent.com/pod-product-compliance
Lightning Source LLC
Chambersburg PA
CBHW020806230426
43666CB00007B/887